TALL TALES
OF A SHORT CLOWN

by Barry Lubin

Copyright 2014 Barry Lubin
All Rights Reserved.

ISBN: 978-0-9910330-2-7
Library of Congress Control Number: 2014901549

All rights reserved. No part of this book may be reproduced or transmitted in any form or by any means, electronic or mechanical, including photocopying, recording, or by any information storage and retrieval system, without permission in writing from the publisher or author.

Cover Credits
Cover Photo: Maike Schulz
Cover & Interior Design: Kevin Hill
Grandma Says Cartoon: Art by Rocco Paris

First Published by AuthorMike Ink, TBA
www.AuthorMikeInk.com

AuthorMike Ink and its logos are trademarked by AuthorMike Ink.

Printed in the United States of America

CHAPTERS

Foreword 1
Prologue – A Brief History Of Grandma 2
Clown College 6
My Mom, My Dad, My Ex, My Bro, My Plane Crash 13
Lovers And Townies 28
Paul Newman 32
Titles My Publisher Turned Down 34
Pass It Forward 40
Sobriety, Elephants, And Losing The Funny 46
Celebrities I Have Pissed Off 54
Being In The Zone 64
The Big C And Me 68
Seeing The World On Someone Else's Dime 79
Failures 81
Regrets 88
Fame 90
Fans 100
Baby You Can Drive My Grandma 104
Anecdotes And Near Death Experiences 111
Semester At Sea Fall 2012 126
I Fell In Love All Over Again 133
The Clown Walks Away 138
Ten People Who Made A Difference/Heroes 140
Epilogue 152
Acknowledgments 153

Foreword

I am Grandma the Clown. If I weren't Grandma, I would probably be writing about my life as a dentist. A respectable career, but not as respectable as wearing a dress for a living.

My bobble head. Photo by David Wallack

What you are about to read is the story of a short guy from a small town who took the road less traveled and ended up in the International Clown Hall of Fame.

On this journey you will discover that the man under the dress is a clown, circus performer, world traveler, recovering alcoholic, actor, father, lover, friend, flirt, director, egomaniac, dancer, bastard, cynic, mentor, bodysurfer, writer, boring eater, and teacher.

I figured I had a book somewhere inside of me, because how many people do you know who can say they sat in Gene Kelly's lap; got to know Isabella Rossellini; hugged Paul Newman; pissed off Meryl Streep; rode elephants; got laughs on six continents; headlined a stand-up comedy club in Stuttgart, Germany; sailed up the Amazon; hung out with an astronaut and a princess and a U.S. Ambassador; put a shower cap on Robert De Niro; was snubbed by Steven Sondheim; and raised two remarkable and lovely daughters…all because of a red dress, gray wig, and carpet bag? I may be the only one who qualifies.

I hope you enjoy reading it half as much as I enjoyed writing it. I actually hope you enjoy it twice as much. Actually, I hated every second, so maybe you will love it. On second thought, enjoy.

Prologue - A Brief History of Grandma

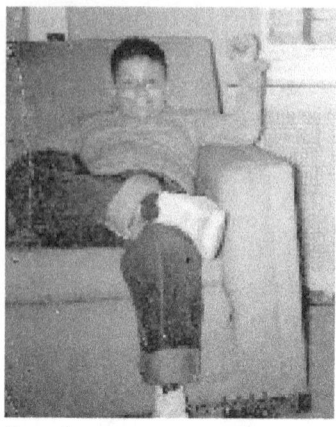

Young Barry

1952. My character, Grandma, was born out of desperation on January 1, 1975, in Venice, Florida. How she is always older than me is a real mystery. I was on my first professional gig with the Ringling Brothers and Barnum & Bailey Circus – the Red Unit, specifically. In December, we rehearsed for the opening of the show. During breaks, the clowns would rush back to an area known as Clown Alley and work on their "walk-arounds" – simple sight gags played on the hippodrome track, which was the rubber matt-covered area that surrounded the three rings. All twenty-eight clowns were expected do a sight gag, where they would then move to a different spot on the track, repeat the gag, and continue until the ringmaster's whistle blew, indicating the next act was ready to begin.

While everyone was working on their walk-around gags, I was at a complete loss as to what to do. I wanted to do something funny, but what, how, in what character? I felt a certain sense of fear that I was "behind in my work" and wouldn't make the cut if I didn't come up with something pretty damn quick. I watched my fellow clowns day after day running off to the clown area to rehearse, and I had nothing. I became a bit desperate, and out of that desperation, I came up with an idea involving a little old man character. As I was thinking about what I could do as an old man, I realized that, inevitably, I would be compared to a character that was then starring in the biggest show on television, Laugh In. Arte Johnson was doing a

Middle School, Ventnor, NJ, If you find the girl who is third from the left in the front row, I am directly behind her in the back row.

dirty little old man character that was always lusting after women. Arte was so popular at the time that comparison was inevitable. Frustrated, but still liking the idea of playing an "old" character, I figured I'd try an old lady character.

Little did I know it would change my life forever.

I had the idea of an old lady, but, now what? I thought about a gag I had learned during Clown College and adapted it to the character. I decided that I would take an oval makeup mirror, which was a large-handled prop with no mirror so the audience could see my face as I "looked" at myself. The gag was simple: look at my face, indicate I need a little something to look better, take out my own "powder sock" (an old sock filled with baby powder used to powder my clown makeup), bash my face repeatedly with it until my face was completely white, look back in the prop mirror, indicate I like what I see, then spit out teeth in the form of white rice.

With an idea of the character, I now needed an outfit. In Clown College I was encouraged to make my own costume – learn to design it, sew it, and repair it myself. So of course I ignored that advice and went to the Salvation Army to buy the outfit in its entirety. I found a carpet bag big enough to hold huge props, and a red winter coat, which reminded me of the little old ladies I would see sitting outside in Miami Beach when I vacationed there in high school. I remember thinking it was funny that in eighty-degree weather they wore winter coats, but now that I am older I understand why. I found funny red sneakers, white beads, and clip-on earrings. These purchases were done on the fly, because the clowns who had given me a lift up to the store were done shopping, and they were getting very impatient.

At the time I had curly hair and plenty of it styled in a Jewish afro, so I thought I would just baby powder my hair until it looked grayish-white. To finish off the look, I added yellow knee-high socks that I had from my regular clown costume. That was the look of Grandma on day one. I liked the look; the only problem was having so much baby powder in my hair that every time I turned my neck, a white cloud would emanate from my head.

January 1: Show number one, day number one of my career and new life. Shortly after the opening production number, it was time for us clowns to do our walk-around gags. This is when I debuted Grandma. I walked onto the arena floor in super slow motion. Part of the reason was to look entirely different from the two-dozen clowns who had sprinted out to get the first laughs. I also chose to look like someone pedestrian, rather than grandiose, to stand out among them by being different. Most of the look on Ringling clowns was loud plaids, stripes, colorful wigs, and big shoes, so a red dress and purse was far from the norm. And it worked. The audience's reaction was immediately apparent. To the crowd, it looked like one of them had accidentally left the audience and ended up in the circus. People were pointing at me. The fact that most of the audience in Florida looked like Grandma helped enormously.

I maneuvered to a spot where no other clown was at that moment – the ones rushing past me were already on their way to their second and third repetition – as I took out the giant yellow prop mirror and did the bit. It got no response at all. I put the mirror back in my big carpetbag, moved down the hippodrome track, and repeated the gag, only now my face was covered in white baby powder from the first time I did the gag. Again…didn't get any response. By then, the ring change was finished, which was the only reason twenty-eight clowns were out there. The whistle blew, which meant I had to get the hell out of there. I refused to break character, so I walked as fast as a hurried old lady could, but that wasn't fast enough. When I got back to clown alley, I was told that the performance director had complained and insisted I not stay out there that long.

What I did learn that day was that I received a lot of attention, regardless of whether I was funny or not, which I was not. Just getting attention among so many clowns was no easy feat, and I knew then and there that I had something with this little old lady character. In Clown College, my master teacher, David Nicksay, talked about the concept of going into the audience before the show to warm up the crowd, and to let them know you. That way, when you appeared later in the show, they'd be excited to see you. He said it would put you at an advantage. I started going into the audience during the pre-show, known as the "come in."

Being sick of inhaling a half-pound of baby powder a day, I'd found a gray wig. I'd also stopped doing the ineffective mirror clown gag, and left my own glasses on for character (and so I could actually see). I began to spend countless hours improvising, playing, and trying little bits in the audience from that point forward.

It was there, in audiences across America, that I learned the character, and it was from there that I got my name. I had yet to think of one at that time, but because so many people called me it when they saw me, I became…Grandma.

Since the beginning, Grandma has always been an outsider in the magical world of the circus, an audience member looking in with wonder. Grandma happens to be lucky enough to enter the ring in order to live out her fantasy of being a graceful, majestic, accomplished circus artist, and naturally she falls far short. It can be viewed in many ways, and often the reviewer, feature writer, and observer will report that Grandma represents the everyman-woman, the ordinary person in search of something greater than themselves. Me, I just am going for laughs, and have been lucky enough to find an international character that resonates with audiences wherever I take her.

The end of Grandma's brief history is the most beautiful part. There is no end. Grandma is an ever-revolving character. There is a great deal of me in her, and her in me. My wonderful instructors talked a great deal about the difference between stepping into a role as an actor and bringing out my real personality traits, feelings, and passions with my clown character. It is truly an "inside job" – mining the real me, doing a psychological analysis of who I really am, and in a way, choosing to expose the real me to the public. I like to call Grandma the best of Barry. I can and I do choose to use a lot of my real self, but not all. It isn't really necessary to do so, and it may even do the audience a disservice to show all of me, via this or any other character, but I can assure you: there is a lot of me in every performance. This also means that Grandma has grown and changed over the decades, just as Barry has. My next performance will always be a compilation of all the experiences I have had in a wig and a dress since January 1, 1975.

I enjoy playing Grandma now more than ever, and I will continue to play Grandma as long as it continues to be a blast. Grandma is my gift, my legacy, and the vehicle I have invented to give my love to the world.

Helping old ladies across the street is great unless you are in the subway

Clown College

My circus life began at Ringling Brothers and Barnum & Bailey Clown College – yes, a college for clowns – though my clowning life began much earlier in the years when I realized that doing pratfalls, mimicking people, and being a pest got me a lot of attention. I remember getting my first big laugh when I made a mistake in third grade and then acted like I was kidding. I was asked by my teacher what "am" and "not" might form as a contraction, and I said, "amn't." The class laughed. I was really embarrassed, but I liked the attention and acted like I did it on purpose. When classmates told me how funny that was, I knew I was on to something. I eventually learned to mimic people for laughs, and could do various accents to get a chuckle (which for some reason I now suck at). Then there was an incident with a phone booth when I was around ten years old. I was riding my bicycle with some friends on the boardwalk in my hometown of Ventnor, New Jersey, and accidentally crashed into a large glass phone booth. I went up and over the

My Ringling Clown College Class of 1974 photo, I am looking sideways, second row, nearly all the way to the left, red polka dot hat. RINGLING BROS. AND BARNUM & BAILEY TM images courtesy of Feld Entertainment, Inc. RINGLING BROS. AND BARNUM & BAILEY * *and THE GREATEST SHOW ON EARTH* * *are owned and used by permission of Ringling Bros. - Barnum & Bailey Combined Shows, Inc. Courtesy of Feld Entertainment*

handlebars, slammed into the phone booth, and hurdled onto the wooden boardwalk. My friends were laughing their asses off. As I picked myself up, I realized I wasn't hurt in the least. And while I was a bit embarrassed, I loved the attention. So much so that I decided to do it again…this time on purpose. Again, I got the same result. I flew over the handlebars, landed with relatively no pain, and again my friends laughed their asses off. A clown was born… or an idiot.

In high school, my friend, Marc Koltnow, who was far funnier than me, told me about a prestigious institute of higher learning…for clowns. I thought it was interesting at the time, but never seriously thought of pursuing it, as being a clown wasn't a "real job." I needed to go to school to get real education. With this theory in my brain, I went off to Boston to attend Emerson College…which didn't last long. After dropping out in 1973, I took a year off to "find myself." This deep soul searching led me to a less than gratifying job as a bill collector.

In between harassing people to pay their electric bill, I saw an ad in the newspaper saying Ringling was playing downtown at the Boston Garden. Recalling the school, I looked at the list of delinquent bills I had yet to call on and decided Clown College was a much more interesting path in life. Sneaking in some personal calls, I found out that they were holding auditions for the college. I asked the boss at the collection agency for the afternoon off (lying about having to deal with an issue at my apartment) to go and audition.

With my gut in knots, unsure if this was something I could do, or wanted to do, I went down to the Boston Garden. Entering the arena and seeing the rings set up, the rigging spread out, and performers practicing, I wish I could tell you that I felt right at home, but I experienced something quite different. It was a world I knew nothing about, but it was fascinating. After a blur of being ushered from one table to another, I was casually introduced to a young woman, who was also auditioning, and then paired off with an experienced clown named Jim Howle. I felt like an outsider and I wanted to run, but after a few jokes, he made both of us feel right at home in the circus ring. Jim shared his experiences with the two of us and answered lots of questions. Hearing his stories actually made me want to be in that ring. After some practice and tips from Jim, I auditioned. The skit I did was a pantomime of a tightrope walker, which I had to do in front of the Dean of Clown College,

Bill Ballantine. He worked with me on it a few times, and at the end of my little mime piece, he looked at me with his piercing blue eyes, gazing intensely, and said, "All right." While Clown College was tougher to get into than Harvard Law School (different set of applicants, I believe, though some at Harvard might disagree), those two words somehow gave me the confidence that I would be invited to the school that fall.

Three months after being fired from my bill-collecting job, I went back home to Ventnor and took a job driving a taxi. It was a thankless and boring job, but an easy one, and it earned me a bit of money while still trying to "find myself." One day, while parked on a quiet side street reading a paper and waiting for a pick-up, the dispatcher crackled over the radio, saying, "Barry, call home." For a second my heart dropped, but then the static broke with, "It's good news, not bad." At that moment I knew that I had gotten into Clown College.

In the late summer of 1974, I packed my bags and headed to Venice, Florida – a sleepy retirement town on the Gulf of Mexico. The taxi driver let me off at the office of the Venice Villas that boiling hot day in August, and the place was already in full swing with my fellow classmates, all who obviously had far more talent than me to have qualified for entrance. How did I know this? Within view of the office, people were doing double-backward somersaults off the high diving board into the pool, several people were juggling more objects than I had ever imagined possible, and several more were doing daring acrobatics on the lawn adjacent to the pool. I knew how to juggle three balls (poorly), was afraid of heights, and had never taken a gymnastics class in my life. I truly felt like there was no place for me in that world – that this was the wrong decision. It was a shock to my system. After my audition with Bill Ballantine, the Dean of Clown College, I really wanted to experience this world, but suddenly I felt certain that I should have turned around right then and there and gone back to New Jersey, or back to Boston for my senior year at Emerson College. Instead, I swallowed my pride (and possibly common sense), and stayed.

Those of us who were lucky enough to be part of this "institution of lower learning," as we liked to call it, were transformed from mild-mannered citizens to…clowns. The school was designed for one simple reason: to create and nurture new talent

1976 Ringling Brothers Clown Alley
RINGLING BROS. AND BARNUM & BAILEY TM images courtesy of Feld Entertainment, Inc. RINGLING BROS. AND BARNUM & BAILEY ® and THE GREATEST SHOW ON EARTH ® are owned and used by permission of Ringling Bros. - Barnum & Bailey Combined Shows, Inc. Courtesy of Feld Entertainment

to be circus clowns for the two traveling units of Ringling Brothers and Barnum & Bailey. We all took classes in makeup and costume design, stilt walking, elephant riding, juggling, balancing, wire-walking, acrobatics, tumbling, human pyramids, circus history, and trampoline. It was an extensive, in-depth curriculum on the art of clowning; each night, after the grueling physical days in the Florida heat, we even studied classic silent films starring some of the great physical comedians.

Venice Arena was a former airplane hangar, which was converted into a circus arena capable of holding three rings of "The Greatest Show on Earth." It was there we rehearsed and did some performances in front of a live audience. It was humid and dusty, yet just about the most exciting place I had ever been in my entire life. It buzzed with life when Clown College and the circus were in town. When it was quiet, dust gathered, and only the famous logo on the outside of the arena gave any hint to passersby that this was indeed a very special place.

Over the course of the next eight weeks, my classmates and I were taught by a very talented faculty, many of whom were clowns from the touring units of Ringling. Some of the other instructors were incredible performers in a variety of skills. I took mime, dance, and movement classes; got hoisted up onto an elephant; attempted to throw a backward somersault on a trampoline; tried to walk on six-foot stilts; learned to sew costumes; and more. Oddly, the one class I was horrible at was clown makeup. I was actually so bad with the motor skills necessary for putting on the greasepaint that I thought I might get kicked out of the school. Eventually, with a lot of help, tons of practice, and a few million clogged pores, I figured out the best way to cover my face in an array of experimental clown faces until I found my "face."

The best part of school was meeting some of the finest people I have ever had the privilege and pleasure of getting to know, many of whom I have kept in contact with since, and whom I still consider great friends. I was introduced to the people who became my heroes, and was treated to the finest education any clown in the world could get in eight weeks, tuition free.

Two young punks from Ringling days, me and Jimmy Tinsman

A good friend who never went to Clown College often said to me that he hated it when various graduates talked about our shared experience when he was around. It seemed so "inside," and he felt so "outside." I knew exactly what he meant, and I am so proud to be one of the insiders. When I was inducted into the Sarasota Ring of Fame in January of 2012, I real-

The instructors of Clown College and me, meeting my hero, Jerry Lewis! Madison, Wisconsin. When he found out us clowns wanted to say hello, he visited with us for an hour!

ized what a great honor it was to also be the very first graduate of Clown College to be inducted, knowing how many great clowns preceded me and graduated after me.

At the 30th Anniversary Reunion of Clown College, I was "roasted." It was the first and only time it had happened to me and it was a great honor. This reunion was held in Baraboo, Wisconsin – known for being the founding place of the Ringling Brothers Circus, and still home to the Circus World Museum and now the International Clown Hall of Fame. However, leading up to the reunion, I had something else on my mind: I'd just found out that I had thyroid cancer. Right after the event, I was to have my thyroid removed, so my stress level and emotions were running high. This event, which I liked to call therapy, couldn't have come at a better time: I desperately needed distraction and laughter. I can honestly say I have never laughed that hard in my life, as one after another of my dear friends and colleagues made unbridled fun of me, my habits, my career, my weakness for tuna sandwiches and bagels, and many other items. I went through half a box of Kleenex crying from laughing so hard.

At Emerson College in 1970 doing my pantomime to the song, Cobwebs and Strange, by The Who

Provided for the roast was a drummer to do accents and drum hits on punch lines. He looked ridiculously young. Part of me felt bad that he was being subjected to the filthiest words ever created. When it was my turn, I looked over at him and asked his age. When he said fourteen, I then uttered the F-bomb around ten times in a row. I figured that would take the onus off any further foulness or cussing, of which there was, and would be, plenty.

To be so honored was a surprise to me when I found out about it before the reunion, but one I embraced with joy and fear at the same time. It was fantastic and therapeutic in ways nearly no one there knew at the time. Of course, the roast never would have been possible had it not been for good old Clown College.

Not only did the school provide new talent for the two road companies of Ringling, but it was a public relations feast as well, creating lots of national and local press, as well as television hits for the company. Any time a clown was accepted, the local press was more than happy to cover this kind of good news, and when a clown was lucky enough to be hired for one of the traveling units of the circus – whenever he or she was in or near his hometown – the press coverage was always tremendous and positive. Win-win for clown and company.

During school, I was changed in ways that I hadn't anticipated, and I owe much to Irvin and Kenneth Feld's generosity. They birthed me, encouraged the creative process, and provided enormous show business experience and lessons, which I still apply and pass along all the time. My training was brief – just eight weeks – but those two months launched me. Whenever people from professional acting or circus and clown schools realize how short the course was for Clown College, they are shocked and then they laugh at the absurdity of trying to learn an art form in such a brief time. But the reality is, I learned on the job. My great instructors, from David Nicksay, to Lou Jacobs, to Bobbie Kaye, to Hovey Burgess, gave me the tools to go out into the vast arenas of America and learn the craft of circus clowning for myself. I dedicated myself to doing the work, one baby step at a time – always changing, developing, learning, and taking risks. The value of my experience taught me that comedy failure doesn't kill – it just hurts, and the sun always rises the next day.

The producers of Ringling Brothers and Barnum & Bailey, Irvin and Kenneth Feld, had started Clown College for the purpose of creating new clowns for their shows, but their real contribution is incalculable. Through their dedication to bringing quality entertainment to millions, they created a family tree of entertainers that has spread throughout the world, touching countless lives, and spreading happiness. With over twelve hundred clowns birthed in the school's thirty years, it would be impossible to create a number high enough to count all the laughs and smiles that were a product of their brilliant invention. The world could use more smiles, and clowns to help bring them out; thankfully, Clown College helped the world in that department for quite a while.

> To err is human, to make mistakes is pretty similar.

My Mom, My Dad, My Ex, My Kids, My Bro, My Plane Crash

In a person's life, there are many influential players, often the most important being family. They are the ones who shape our view of the world at the start, and that influence lasts a lifetime. I will share a bit of my background here, though I do it with trepidation. I warned my kids about this chapter and told them I would be gentle. My daughters, Danielle and Emily, are the gentlest of all my family, and have helped and supported me for their entire lives. What do they say? Child is father to the man? So true. They also say: behind every great man is a great woman. And behind every great woman is a great man. What's behind every man who dresses like a woman? My kids!

My mom, Edythe Lee Weinberg Lubin, was born in Camden, New Jersey, on March 6, 1921, to Myrtle and Myron Weinberg. She was very proud of me for becoming what I became: her mother. Okay, that may not properly describe it, but my Grandma character was fashioned a bit after my own Grandma, Nana Wein-

Me and Danielle Lubin during a rehearsal of Big Apple Circus, circa 1986. Photo by Bert Lubin

Chuck Burnes, me with Danielle Lubin 1988, Los Angeles. Photo by Bert Lubin

berg. My mom wasn't thrilled that I joined the circus, thinking it was a temporary diversion and that I would eventually find a "real job." I was often annoyed with her question of when was I going to finally get a real job, but it was understandable since she was a Jewish mother. The circus was not in our vocabulary at home, and the idea of my career being some silly show you paid a few bucks to see on a Saturday afternoon was a very foreign concept to her. In fact, it was quite a foreign concept to me, too, which was part of the appeal during my early twenties when I was unsure of my life and career.

I will never forget the phone call she made to my dispatcher when I was driving that cab in Atlantic City. The dispatcher relayed the message, "Cab 52, call your mother. She said it's good news, not bad." The memory of that moment never fails in causing me to tear up, as it was the moment my path in life had changed. I was a college dropout, living at home, driving a cab in the dying town of Atlantic City (pre-gambling), worried about my lack of direction. That was somehow all right at Emerson College, but this was real life, and my six-days-a-week, twelve-hours-a-day job driving a taxi was making a big impression…on my ass. That call was a lifesaver.

1991 with my family and Katherine Binder. Photo by Tisha Tinsman

For the first two decades of my career, Mom continued to ask me when I was going to get a real job. Finally, she came to realize that I was no longer asking to borrow money, and that my wife and children were not destitute, and actually well fed and clothed by my circus career. The tipping point for my mom was the first time I appeared on The Today Show on NBC. All of a sudden, she was telling the neighbors, her friends, and all of our family how proud she was of her son, the circus clown, who was on national television!

She had seen me live just a couple of times with Ringling Brothers when I had small roles in the show. I remember a surreal feeling as I sat on an elephant waving at her, thinking she must be impressed with me, but at the same time knowing she must be scared shitless that her son was on top of such a huge non-kosher beast. (Jews do not eat elephant. Bacon, yes.) She was very conservative about safety and it had to be tough on her watching me ride hands free on a freakin' elephant…wearing makeup. Then I brought her to Lincoln Center when I was starring in a Big Apple Circus show in the cultural center of New York City, next to the New York City Ballet, the Metropolitan Opera, and the New York Philharmonic. Grandma was on a huge banner facing Broadway in front of Lincoln Center, and to bring my mom to New York to see that made me so happy. I like to think she was very proud of me.

Mom was the type of Jewish mother who may have thought no girl was good enough for me, but my wife at the time, Roberta, was a real saint to Edythe, having nursed her back to health twice when she had debilitating injuries. Though

Katherine Binder and Danielle Lubin. Photo by Tisha Tinsman

she may not have loved my choice at first, she grew to love Roberta and appreciated her role in the family as both mom and artist. My mother passed away just a week before rehearsals started in 2001 for Big Apple Circus, and I closed up her home, selling or donating everything in one week's time. Without a break, I went into rehearsals. I felt emotionally crippled – mostly because I had been with Mom during her decline – which, thankfully, was only bad the last two weeks of her life. I tried my best to comfort her, and felt terrible that we hadn't gone to Scandinavia before she became too weak to travel. It was her greatest wish to see the north countries of Europe. (Ironically, I now live in Sweden.) She was so scared during her decline, I remember helping her through some of this fear by telling her, whether I believed it myself or not, that soon she would be with her deceased mom, Myrtle, to whom she was very close before her death. Mom and Nana Weinberg used to talk on the phone for hours each day, and I think the idea comforted Mom to wonder about the reunion that would soon take place in heaven.

Mom wanted to die at home, and we arranged a hospital bed to be placed in the living room so she wouldn't have to climb steps to her bedroom. A hospice worker was also hired. I was there when Mom passed. As I left her house that day, I realized I was an orphan.

I spread her ashes in the Atlantic Ocean by the street where we had lived. I found out that it is illegal to do so on a public beach, so I placed her ashes in a colorful child's plastic sand bucket I purchased for the occasion, waded into the warm August sea up to my knees, and spread them in the place my brother Jay and I felt she would have loved the most: Derby Avenue Beach in Ventnor. A month later, 9/11 shocked New York City and the entire world, and in a way, I was grateful Mom didn't have to witness that horror in her time on earth. As the ashes floated away, I thought of the countless days she spent playing with us on that beach.

My brother, Jay, and I are polar opposites in some ways, yet very similar in others. Jay was a career Navy officer and retired as a captain with a pension after thirty years in the military. A Navy officer and a man who puts on dresses are on very two different career paths. Jay was a brilliant student who got into a very-hard-to-get-into college. I was lame, but I got into a good school. He was an exceptional boy scout. I barely passed any tests for merit badges and was never able to make a fire by myself. He lived a very comfortable life as a leading executive in an insurance company, and he and his wife, Linda, raised two kids beautifully: my nephew, Adam, and my niece, Laura. I led and still lead a relatively uncomfortable life in terms of creature comforts, due to travel and a not-so-secure business, but my ex and I also managed to raise two kids beautifully. Jay is married; I am divorced. He is in the business of business; I am in the business of pleasure. The last time we spent significant time together was just before our mom passed away. I regret not seeing him and his family more, but Sweden is a little ways from Connecticut. I love him. And I hope he knows that.

My dad, George Simon Lubin, was born in Philadelphia, Pennsylvania, on May 12, 1926, to Sidney and Anne Rabinowitz Lubin. George was a charming and funny guy who used humor in his work quite a lot. He gave a number of speeches and always seemed to bring down the house. He even sold our house that way, creating a very funny radio ad that brought a ton of people to our home to take a look. He often took me to work with him, and I always admired how strong he was when lifting heavy equipment. After high school, he was accepted to UCLA to study becoming a film director, but he never made it to Los Angeles. He made too much money doing his summer job, which was renting sound and projection equipment, and showing films for hotel guests in Atlantic City. He made it into his year-round business, which expanded and thrived. While living in a great part of Ventnor, the town neighboring Atlantic City, we owned several airplanes and the best car money could buy. My mom always said we lived above our means, but Dad managed to give us a very high quality of life.

On the other hand, Dad always promised the family exciting trips around the U.S. to national parks and big cities, but we never actually went. Why, I do not know. We did, however, make one vacation trip with Dad's plane to Cape Cod, a place that interested him and Mom because of the Kennedy Clan. We basically hung out at the motel pool for four days, but it was still a lot of fun. The most interesting part of that trip was the very end, when we survived our airplane's crash landing. As we approached the airport in Atlantic City, the pilot had attempted to lower the landing gear, but it was stuck in a partly deployed position. He knew it had the potential to be bad, and he prepared us for crash positioning inside the plane. He stalled the engine close to the ground, and we landed with no injuries. When we got out of the plane and saw by the tire marks just how short our landing had been, a total skid mark of twelve feet in length, we knew we were very lucky. Mom wasn't too happy about flying after that. Another thing Mom wasn't happy about: after the crash, I began taking flying lessons from Dad. I was actually doing take-offs and flights (but no landings), with him as my co-pilot. Once their divorce was final, she forbade me from ever flying with him again.

Perhaps it was the time I got to spend in projection booths with Dad at various resort hotel theaters in Atlantic City that I remember most vividly. For two summers, my dad rented the Quarterdeck Theater in an old resort hotel to show silent movies. Nearly no one came, but I loved being introduced to Charlie Chaplin and Buster Keaton and Harold Lloyd and others this way. Night after night, my job was to rewind the reels of film when they finished, and when I wasn't doing that, I looked through the tiny window inside the projection booth at the movies up on the big screen. I loved it. I couldn't have predicted how valuable that experience would be until I became a silent comedian myself. Little did I know that I was doing research at a very young age. When I was 22, we were required as Clown College students to train all day, and after dinner we would come back to the Venice Arena to watch silent films and study physical comedy. I knew these films so well that I was able to sleep during the showings and still ace every test.

At times, my dad rented more adult-themed movies (what we would now consider R-rated), to entertain summer hotel guests in Atlantic City. All those films, and the 16-millimeter projector which played them, would come home, and I was allowed to watch the films before he had to return them to the film rental company. I watched some of the greatest film comedians, from Jerry Lewis, to Laurel & Hardy, to the great Jack Lemon and Tony Curtis, and I secretly dreamed of being them as I watched their films over and over again. When I met Jerry Lewis a few years ago, I told him how much he had influenced me in my work. I wish I had shared with him exactly how I had been exposed to his genius.

I remember reading the Sunday edition of The New York Times at home, especially the Arts and Leisure section, and secretly dreaming of being in those pages one day. That dream became a reality when I was reviewed dozens of times, and featured in articles about my life and my career. My dream of being in the movies was also realized, but you would be hard-pressed to find me in any of them, which include Woody Allen's Alice, My Life, starring Michael Keaton and Nicole Kidman, and Big Top Pee-Wee, starring Pee-wee Herman. My friend, Marc Koltnow, owned a video rental store and whenever I hung out there with him he would tell customers that I was in the movies. This would always intrigue them. Then Marc would slip one of "my movies" in the VCR, find the two seconds I was in, and stop the frame so I could be seen. Every time, the customer wouldn't even believe it was me.

It was 1981 when an obituary in the Atlantic City Press informed me of my father's passing in Las Vegas, where he had been living. I was estranged from him at the time of his death, but was planning a trip to Las Vegas to try to make amends, to rekindle our relationship, to do whatever I could to become his son again. Dad loved me a lot. He called me his "Schnookie," and I always knew how he felt about me, until things changed when I was fourteen and my parents divorced. My mom used me as a pawn to garner information about him and his finances. He knew it, his mom – my Nana Lubin – knew it, and they both seemed to stop loving me at that time. It was a very tough and strange period in my life, and I found myself drawing away from my emotions, which I could neither handle nor comprehend, the worst of which was the feeling of abandonment.

I cannot describe how awful and terribly lonely I felt. It burned so deeply that I have been running from that pain ever since. I felt that the most important man in my life no longer loved me. Perhaps that's what led me to abuse drugs and alcohol later in my life. Perhaps it was a way to fill the void. That fear still plagues me, and perhaps it even informs me subconsciously of how to live day to day.

With my brother, Jay Lubin and my niece Laura Lubin. Do you see the resemblance_ Photo by Linda Lubin.

I have lived my life making sure I would never do that to my children. I never want them to suffer that pain. It became my father's job to forgive me and love me unconditionally, but it was not to be. I regret that he passed away just a few weeks before my last effort to try to bring our relationship back from the dead. And I have never properly grieved that loss. I probably can't.

I went to Las Vegas just after his death on a pleasure trip… with a purpose. I knew of his last address and that he had a daughter, Anne, from his second marriage, who I hadn't seen since she was a toddler. I wanted to see her and ask where my father was buried, so I could begin the grieving process. I took a cab to the house, not knowing if anyone from the family still lived there, and rang the doorbell. No answer. Rang it again. No answer. For some reason, I stood at the door for an unreasonably long time. After a while I heard a voice from inside ask, "Who is it?" Through the door I replied that I was George Lubin's son. The voice asked, "Barry?" Anne opened the door and we talked there for a little while, quite uncomfortably, until she invited me in.

Anne told me that her mom and dad, throughout her life, had hidden the fact that she had five half-brothers, and it was only after his death that she found out about them. Subsequently, she had met her mother's three sons with mixed results, and had just guessed through the door that I was Barry and not my brother, Jay. She was not happy that her parents had hidden so much from her, but she was on a quest to find her family and fill in the missing pieces.

After a while, I asked where our father was buried. She showed me an urn on the mantle above the fireplace. My heart dropped. I didn't know what to do. A friend had suggested to me that I go to his grave and talk to him, or if that wasn't possible, that I sit across from an empty chair and talk to my dad as a way of grieving. I felt that I couldn't sit in a relative stranger's house and have a conversation with my dead father while that stranger watched. I left in a semi-daze with lots of swirling emotions. To this day, I feel that I still have not properly grieved the loss of my father, but Anne and I still communicate and often talk about him. Perhaps that is a way of healing.

After his death, I learned that my father invented the prototype for a technology known as the Cuemaster Q 8, which has since become standard in every theater in the world. The system enabled him, with the press of a button, to do multiple sound, light, and projection cues at the same moment. I found this out when I was doing a corporate entertainment job with the Big Apple Circus and one of the techies asked me if I was related to George Lubin. When I told him he was my father, he suddenly acted quite reverent toward me, and he was surprised to hear that I didn't know my father had invented this technology now used worldwide. Dad produced large corporate events in Las Vegas and created this to simplify his life instead of doing it all by hand, cue by cue. He never patented it.

Dad never saw me work, which I felt was a tragedy since he had so much influence on my life and my career. He loved the silent comedians, so if I could have made him laugh, it would have meant the world to me. A conversation I had with my half-sister changed all that: she told me that she and my dad had been watching a national television show together, on which I was appearing, and she heard my name and asked Dad if he knew a Barry Lubin… His answer to her was no, but somehow, the knowledge that he had seen my work really warmed my heart.

You may ask yourself: how can a father abandon two sons? Unbelievable, unforgivable. I am still trying to find a way to heal, forgive him, understand, and move on.

Dad was funny, and I admired him for that and many other things, but he was also full of promises he made to his family that he didn't keep. I was not the best father, but I always loved my daughters and always will, and they know it. I made sure we traveled quite a lot, my younger much less due to her fear of flying long distances over the ocean. My older daughter, Danielle, is a great traveler, and we have had numerous international adventures together for circus and for fun. I hope I provided memories for them that are very different from the ones between my dad and me. I moved to Sweden in 2011, and I come back to the U.S. to see them as often as possible. I hope to God they never feel that I abandoned them by moving to Europe.

My kids grew up around the circus and circus people. That allowed them to view the world in a different way than many children, most of that in a good way. They came to know people and cultures from around the world, getting to know Bulgarians, Chinese, Russians, South Americans, Swiss, Kenyans, South Africans, Canadians, and so many others. They were able to enjoy and appreciate human relationships with the most amazing animals on earth, including majestic, intelligent, and beautiful elephants. Our cats, Flipper and Rover, reacted more than my kids did when an elephant would saunter by our trailer, but Danielle and Emily loved and appreciated them, along with horses, dogs, camels, goats, and whatever else was under the Big Top any given season. It is interesting what becomes commonplace to one and novelty to others. To a child whose father is a plumber, big wrenches and plungers are the norm. The child of an office worker is familiar with pressed suits or dresses, briefcases, and good grooming. To my kids, sawdust, roaring circus audiences, and a father who put on clown makeup, a wig, and a dress every day was their normal. It still is.

Danielle was born on March 9, 1985, and the event was life altering. One of the first things a friend of mine said was, "Oh wow, a girl! Just wait until boys start calling." I said, "What the hell, she isn't even a day old! Shut up!" Danielle suffered a bit from our lack of money in her early years, to the point that she has some trouble enjoying spending what she earns now. We were doing better financially when her sister, Emily, came along, and though we tried to be equitable with the girls, perhaps it still appeared not quite fair to Danielle. She is a clever, dry-humored (like me) beautiful young woman. She is very artistic and very intelligent, which must be hard to deal with when you have both parts of your brain so well developed. (I just have the artistic side to worry about.) Danielle tried various universities and found herself to be somewhat allergic to college, but is now on a path that she loves.

When Danielle was young, she and I developed an act during which I chose a "volunteer" from the audience to help. It was a real volunteer most of the time, but whenever Danielle traveled with me or came out to see a show I was in, I would choose her and she would always bring down the house with her natural acting ability and perfect timing. She made her "professional" circus debut in 1990 in the Big Apple Circus doing an appearance with her friend, Katherine Binder (daughter of Paul Binder, founder of Big Apple Circus), and I told her I would pay her ten cents per show. She still hounds me that I rarely paid her most of the time. Showing early signs of being a real trouper, Danielle never missed a show the entire season.

When we chose to get off the road in 1992, Danielle was seven years old, and we settled in a small town in North Jersey. I thought it might help ease her transition into small-town suburban school life by pointing out to her school and new classmates that Danielle had been in the circus. This immediately backfired, and instead her new classmates taunted her and nicknamed her, not lovingly, "Circus Girl."

Danielle and I had quite a few traveling adventures together. Our first trip together was a little Florida vacation when she was around eight years old. I don't remember a lot about that trip, other than it was a really nice chance to hang out and enjoy some Florida fun and sun; we even went to Weeki Wachee Springs to see real "mermaids."

The next time we traveled together was also her first adventure in Europe. As part of my job with Big Apple Circus, I was occasionally sent to scout talent at one of the big circus festivals. For this particular assignment, we ended up in Paris. Danielle was fourteen, and we attended lots of shows and we saw lots of Paris sights. She was independent enough to go back and forth to the hotel when she got bored with the schmoozing, which is a big part of the circus business. I think she really enjoyed it, and a free trip to Paris isn't exactly off-putting to most teenagers. I even sneaked her into the famed Crazy Horse Saloon, for which you must be 21 to enter. She thought that was cool as hell.

Then, in 2006, when I was booked to perform in Budapest at the International Circus Festival of Hungary, I asked to bring an assistant as part of the deal. Danielle jumped at the chance, and in January of that year we took off for Budapest. I didn't know how valuable she would prove to be. My last experience performing in Europe had been twenty-nine years before, at the International Circus Festival of Monte Carlo, equivalent to the Academy Awards of the circus world. I often talk about failure being the best motivator

A giant Polaroid photo of Danielle and Emily and me in 1992. Photo by Elsa Dorfman

toward eventual success, and that performance was a great motivator. I failed miserably in front of the biggest circus producers and directors in the world, not to mention Cary Grant, Princess Grace Kelly, and Prince Ranier of Monaco. (If you are going to fail, do it right!) My impending performance at the Hungarian Circus festival would be the first since my last "failure," and I was both excited and frightened to death that I might repeat my poor showing of years earlier. I needed Danielle for moral support, and she not only gave me that boost, but also showed that she had a great eye artistically – something she inherited from her mom, Roberta. Quite often she said, when I was most nervous, "Chill Dad." I chilled. She always knew the right thing to say to me. Danielle once said to me, when she was around six years old and after I told her that I might be leaving the Big Apple Circus, "But dad, people need to see Grandma. You can't leave the circus."

Danielle tried circus arts, acting, music, and many other things, but I believe her love is for art itself. The easel she has chosen lives on people's hands. It's an art that requires a delicate touch and great sensitivity, and she has become a fantastic nail artist. In fact, she was recently named one of the top 24 nail artists in America...in her very first year!

My second daughter, Emily, was born in 1990, and her arrival into the world happened on the evening of December 28. While I was putting on my clown makeup in the dressing room next to Big Apple Circus ringmaster Paul Binder, I heard crying inside my head, so I asked Paul what time it was. He answered that it was 7:15. Later, I found out that was exactly the time Emily was born. Earlier that morning, I had brought my then-wife Roberta to Morristown Memorial Hospital during a blizzard, following a snowplow at twenty miles per hour the whole way there, and this was fol-

Another day in paradise... Photo by Kurt Sikora

lowing the hour it had taken to remove the snow from the car sufficiently enough to drive. It felt like it took us eons to get to Morristown, New Jersey. It was rather out of our way, but we had decided to have Emily in the same place and with the same doctors as Danielle. Dads-to-be are always nervous, but with a blizzard and an essential performance later that day, I was trembling like a plate of Jell-O on top of a shoes-filled dryer.

I was considered indispensable to the Big Apple Circus at the time, which meant I could not miss a performance. You might think that the birth of a child is more important than any job, but in showbiz, the show must go on, even if your wife is in labor.

I immediately regretted asking the lovely people in charge of this fantastic animal to do this photo. Scared the hell out of me! Circus Krone 2007. Photo by Liam Kreal

The plan was this: if Roberta's labor took a while, Charmaine Liddicoat, our friend and the wife of circus general manager, Brian Liddicoat, would drive out to Morristown to coach the birth. That is exactly what happened. That night, during the finale of the show, Paul stopped the performance and announced to the Lincoln Center audience that Grandma was a new dad. (That line still kills me). The audience stood and applauded, and I took off my wig so that the kids could see that I was really a man. I was so overtaken with emotion that I sobbed in front of fifteen hundred people bent over at the waist. After the show, I drove out to Morristown to see my little Emily and sobbed again. There was an article in the New York Post two days later announcing Emily's arrival. And if you asked me now, I would tell you frankly that I wish I had been present at Emily's birth.

Emily followed in her sister's footsteps and performed the act with me as the volunteer coming out of the audience. In one instance, the audience numbered close to twenty thousand in the Skydome in Toronto during a weekend engagement with Garden Brothers Circus. It is one thing to bring down the house with a thousand people in attendance, but twenty thousand is like, well, twenty times as big. During the shows, people went crazy over Emily's simple bits, which Danielle and I had written and developed together. Her sense of timing was impeccable, just like her sister's, and she sensed the crowd's reaction. It was impossible to ignore. Emily wrote a school paper about the experience the following fall, and she called it the highlight of her year. It was certainly one of mine.

Emily is very smart, very sweet, and has a great sense of humor. I had grown up with a high-achieving older brother, to whom I was inevitably compared, so I didn't want my kids to feel they were ever being "compared" to each other (though I am sure we screwed that up from time to time). Emily never seemed to be interested in pursuing a circus or show business career, but we put her in a sleepover camp that specialized in musical theater, and she did an absolutely great job in the musical in which she was cast: "The Sound of Music." She took dance classes for a long time, but the passion wasn't there. Just like her sister, Emily also showed signs of being allergic to college, and has been pursuing a career in retail, managing a well-known clothing store near her home in New Jersey. She is passionate, and is well liked and appreciated in the workplace; we shall see where her journey takes her.

I planned to bring her to Europe for the first time when she was in her early teens. We chose a dream trip to Italy, after taking all her suggestions of the places she wanted to visit. Two weeks before the trip, she told me that she was too scared to fly over the ocean and she declined. I let her know I was disappointed, but I hopefully didn't give her a guilt trip about it. I was heartbroken, but decided to go anyway, and it turned out to be the trip of a lifetime. In Venice, I stayed in a room atop a boutique hotel with my own rooftop terrace. In Rome, I saw the Coliseum and the Forum, and drove down the Amalfi Coast, where I spent a lovely afternoon on the beach in Positano. I had a blast, but I ached every second for what I knew my Emily was missing. I have learned to forgive the little and large stuff when it comes to my kids. My dad taught me the importance of that the hard way.

My ex-wife, Roberta – Bert, as she likes to be called – was

a great dancer, actress, and mother. Early on, we found that we shared a lot in common. We met on Ringling Brothers and Barnum & Bailey's Blue Unit while in rehearsals in Venice, Florida. I had a succession of short romances, with a few longer and more significant ones scattered in, but there came a time when I was ready to settle down. Along came Bert – a beautiful, sexy, feisty, funny, and talented Ringling dancer. We shared a lot of cups of coffee, and soon we were more or less living together…although on a circus train, that wasn't the simplest thing to do. The dancer's car where she stayed had the worst shocks, making every tiny bump feel like a 10.0 earthquake. With Bert's severe motion sickness, this did not lead to many romantic nights as we traversed the country. She ended up needing Dramamine every time we traveled and would eventually pass out, in hopes of just getting the ride over with. On the other hand, to me, the train was the best part of being with Ringling. I would stay up as much as I could to enjoy traveling through the backyards of America.

As a couple, we had a Ka-BLAM of atomic-force chemistry, combusting together and burning brightly. We had an amazing time, and it felt like we were meant for each other. We would often try to escape from the rest of the circus folk by going as far away from the circus as cab or public transportation could take us and find a diner or coffee shop on the road. Inevitably, we would run into the ringmaster and his partner in the same place, which always caused us all to laugh, but we respected each other's need for space. It happened so many times that it became a big joke among the four of us.

I was offered a three-day shoot on a film during the season I met Bert and saw it as a great opportunity for my career. I asked permission to go for three days, but management, and rightly so, refused to give it. I instead chose to quit Ringling, did the three-day shoot, and found myself unemployed. A few weeks later, I returned to visit the Ringling show in San Antonio and I stole Bert away, most certainly before she was ready to leave the circus tour.

Bert and I moved to California, where she had been raised, and though we had our ups and downs, the relationship flourished. I didn't enjoy living there, and I took off for Boston to start my solo stand-up comedy career. While apart, I talked to Bert daily and planned for the day when she would join me, and she did shortly after. We just couldn't be apart. Not long after that, we moved to New York City to continue our pursuit of show business fame and fortune. Bert studied dance and acting, and attended auditions, and I did stand-up comedy, but only briefly. Stand-up in New York City was a very different animal than stand-up in Boston, and I didn't handle it very well. During this time, we went took a trip and got married on July 12, 1981, in Laguna Beach, California, on a cliff overlooking the Pacific.

Reality soon set in, and I ended up doing temporary office work as a survival job, just as I had done in Boston. I missed the circus enormously, so we decided to take in a show at the Big Apple Circus. I fell madly in love with its intimacy with the audience, and its beautiful theatrical shows. Almost instantly I was chasing down leads to get myself in with them. With a lot of persistence, and my Ringling background, I got to be part of a circus I loved. Little did I know how much it would become a part of me for the next thirty years.

After a couple of seasons working there, I asked Paul Binder if Bert might have some skills that would prove useful to the circus. Sure enough, her talent was useful and she was hired in 1984 to be part of the original company, formed to created new acts annually in circus repertory. We moved to Rhinebeck, New York, where she trained to do galloping pyramids on horseback. (I subsequently froze my ass off during this training period.) She had a great time doing bareback riding and pyramids, and even did some clowning with me. Both our careers were starting to flourish, but I managed to screw that up by getting her pregnant. Bert was never in the Big Apple Circus again, something for which I think she never really forgave me. And while our first-born daughter was worth the world to us, losing a career is still hard to take.

Over the years, Bert and I had a harder and harder time staying happy with one another. I take a lot of responsibility for that, and attribute some of it to being absent so much. We struggled, went to marriage counseling, and eventually realized it was not going to work out. It was one of the hardest things I have ever had to deal with. I believed Bert was the love of my life, but it wasn't to be. I felt extremely sad and spectacularly lonely. We separated in 1998 and divorced 15 years later. Don't ask…

All right, you asked.

For 15 years, we were separated with no interest in getting back together. I had a great insurance plan with medical, den-

My first love, Nina Soifer, and the girl with the dot on her nose, Photo by Jill Hatz.

tal, and prescription coverage, and the first lawyer I met after we separated explained that I would have to pay for that once we were divorced. As lame as it may seem, for economic purposes, we remained married so that Bert would continue to be covered, and I would continue not having to pay a ton of money out of my own pocket. My friends would often ask me when I was going to get divorced, but I pointed out that I had moved on and was dating – that I would get a divorce when it made sense. Well, it made sense once I left Big Apple Circus and was no longer on a group insurance plan. Some people thought it was weird, or that I was cheap, but it was neither. We were still friends, she was the mother of my children, and keeping her on my plan was a way for me to take care of them all.

Roberta was instrumental in helping me find some wonderful moments with Grandma. She had great ideas and a wonderful grasp of the character, and together we fashioned many of the pieces I still perform to this day. We get along fine and we are so very proud of our greatest accomplishments together: Danielle and Emily.

In New Jersey, there is a law that states that the separated/divorcing parents must remain friends. It is a totally unenforceable law, but for the kids' sake, it really is a great idea. We managed to remain civil, and I have the utmost respect for her. We have even had Christmas dinner together with our kids, and my girlfriend Ann and one of her kids, Karin.
The world keeps spinning 'round.

Nothing is as fast as a cheetah, but they are only cheetah themselves.

Lovers and Townies

The first girl I kissed was Gloria Lieberman at a party when we were in third grade. We were playing spin the bottle, and Gloria was sweet, cute, and little (like me), so of course I had a crush on her. I remember the kiss as being brief and somewhat uncomfortable, taking place in the closet at someone's home. Regardless, it was amazing, surreal, and the start of my love life.

Nina Soifer was my first real love; I was a senior in high school and she was a freshman. She was cute as a button, quiet, artistic, smart, sensitive, and a great dancer. She clearly made me feel loved, and she still did many years after we broke up when I went off to college. I broke her heart, but I saw it as inevitable at the time. When I was developing my makeup at Clown College in 1974, my instructor, Bobby Kaye, told me we could do something just for ourselves using our clown makeup; Nina had a cute freckle just off center on the tip of her nose, so I added that, and to this day I wear a little black dot there on my painted red nose. People rarely notice it, and it has often been digitally removed from advertisements, as designers think it's a blemish. I wear it to honor her and love itself. I found out that Nina was recently at the dermatologist having some work done on her skin, and without asking, the doctor zapped the dot off her nose before she could stop him.

I still wear mine proudly.

Off to college. Though Emerson College in Boston was overwhelmingly female, I was rarely able to find lovers because I was so uncomfortable in my own skin and just learning about life away from home in the big city for the first time. I lost my virginity a couple of months into my college career with a fellow student and virgin named Alyson, and we both kind of looked at each other afterwards and asked, "Is that it?" I had a great friendship with Casey that occasionally included drunken sex, and there were a

Ann with Richard Gere and me at Big Apple Circus in 2008

few other lovers, but no true love until I was just about gone from Emerson.

Kris was one of the great loves of my life. Our relationship started when we were both at Emerson. She was unlike anyone I had ever imagined. She was worldly, wise, wild, sexy as hell, and we really did fall hard for each other. Then the circus intervened. I fell in love with the circus, too. Each year, when it came time to consider staying with the Ringling Circus or leaving to be with Kris, I chose to stay with the circus. We saw each other quite a lot, and for a short time I moved near her in San Francisco as she attended Mills College in Oakland. I figured I would pursue a career in stand-up comedy while keeping the flame going, but that experiment only lasted a couple weeks. I was living in a transient hotel in the city, and I hated every second. With little money, miserable living conditions, and a poor outlook, I suddenly felt our romance on the wane. Eventually, I had a choice: leave San Francisco or lose my sanity. Though we kept trying to keep the love going, I was too absentee a partner. She found another man, Bennett. I was insanely jealous and in severe pain over this new man in Kris' life and bed.

Kris was the most adventurous woman I had ever met and I just hated the thought that she was sharing new adventures with Bennett. To this day, that name gives me shudders for some reason, though our love affair had run its course decades ago. Young love, incredible chemistry. That horrible feeling of abandonment, which had first reared its ugly head with my dad, reared its head again. Was I true to Kris during the times at Ringling when we were apart? No. But we were discreet and sensible, and realistic, too. Yet, the romance and strong bond never died, and those little flings meant nothing on the scale of what Kris meant to me then. Especially since I had lost her, anyway.

I learned a lot about love, and things that resemble love, once I was a part of "The Greatest Show on Earth." During the rehearsals, there was a great meeting of many people getting to know each other, feeling each other out, becoming familiar with new cultures and new mindsets of people from around the world. Throw in new a cast and crew living together on a train, the difficulties of a short rehearsal period, and long days in the hot arena, and it was incredibly stimulating and incredibly draining, too.

After a few years, I witnessed a fascinating ritual: whenever the new crop of dancers arrived, the acrobats from Europe or South America would swoop in and the young ladies would inevitably swoon at their good looks and exotic accents and cultures. Romance was in the air, and I had learned to just be patient and wait things out. What do I mean by wait things out? Well, with all due respect to good-looking acrobats from other parts of the world, some have a very different way of treating women than many American women are used to. After a short time, somewhere around one month, the girls would often grow tired of the chauvinistic ways of some (but not all) of the acrobats and would defect to the Americans on the show, i.e., the clowns, of which there were an equal number as the dancers.

I may not have had the looks of these acrobats and daring young men, but I had my own charms: mostly that I could make women laugh. That turned out to be a pretty powerful aphrodisiac of its own, overcoming my inability to be tall, dark, handsome, or particularly talented at any circus skill whatsoever. When I met Bert, several were wooing her, but somehow, I was the one who won her heart. We got along splendidly. I think my fellow circus folk were happy for me, knowing I had been a kind of serial romancer (though not what one might call a womanizer) and not very happy at that point. I had done a lot of dating, more for the gratification of my ego than for anything else. I was needy, good at the game, and strategic. In other words, I was a manipulative little bastard.

The local girls from the towns and cities in which we stopped, known in circus parlance as "townies," were often smitten with us circus folk. Typically, the circus train would arrive in a new town on Monday, set up on Monday evening or Tuesday morning, and the circus would open on Tuesday night. That meant I had time to meet a local girl that evening, or possibly on Wednesday, begin "working on them" immediately, and if things worked out, the weekend was blissful. There is something about clowns that some women are prone to fall for – to one degree or another. I could analyze it, but what the hell do I know beyond my own experiences? Suffice it to say, someone coming into your hometown, perhaps not the most exciting place on the planet, and working with a glamorous entity known as "The Greatest Show on Earth", and whose job it is to ride an elephant, or do somersaults forty feet in the air, or walk stilts...well that's intoxicating stuff, isn't it? I am not saying it was like shooting fish in a barrel, but I am saying it was like shooting fish in a barrel. On occasion, a bit more than I had bargained for would come of it, meaning that a young lady might have more feelings for me than I had for her. Great geographical moves across the map often solved that issue, but airplanes do fly from Memphis to Oklahoma, and sometimes I was surprised by a visit in the next town or two towns later. Worse: having to tell someone not to come to the next town on tour, because I didn't have the same feelings for them. To them it was the beginning of a romance. To me, it was just sweet fun.

I was on the other end a couple of times myself, but it never worked out. Geralyn was from Chicago and I was smitten with her. It turns out she was doing from her stationary location what I was doing on tour. Each time the circus came to Chicago, she snagged a hot young man for the few weeks the show was in town. Like a real jerk, I continued to carry her photo in my wallet well into my marriage.

And then there was Debbie in Minneapolis. She was smart, beautiful, funny, and we had a wonderful time together. She flew to me a couple of times and it continued to be quite wonderful, and then I made the mistake of flying to Minneapolis on Valentine's Day to surprise her. When I arrived, it was immediately obvious that it was a bad idea. Without saying it, I knew she had another man, and it was with this man she planned to spend the romantic holiday, not me. She generously let me sleep on her couch, but I didn't see her again. The feeling of being dumped by Debbie was agonizing, because I really cared deeply about her, and it made me feel lonelier than I could remember. It was my own doing, since I didn't call in advance, and just invited myself into her domain. It was not pretty, and that relationship ended on one of the coldest and loneliest Valentine's Days in history.

Ann and I in Lubeck, Germany, shpritzing again, photo by Lars Affeldt

> There is nothing more delicious on this green earth than lava.

Paul Newman

Paul Newman ruined my towel. I am honored to say that. The man was a big fan of the Big Apple Circus; in fact, he quietly donated his Newman's Own Popcorn to the circus for many years. He attended the show regularly, sometimes twice during our annual run at Lincoln Center. His favorite charity, which he founded – the Hole in the Wall Gang – is a small network of camps for kids with serious illnesses and their families. As a fundraiser, they bought out the tent annually, and still do in New York and Boston. Mr. Newman often came for the festivities, which was followed by an auction, in which he played the part of the auctioneer, almost forcing his friends and colleagues to bid high on the items. He also came to the circus for his daughter Clea's charity, Pegasus, which provided horseback riding opportunities for sick and handicapped children. He loved us so much that he wanted to be in the show, so we arranged for him to do a clown routine in the ring during our pre-show. The act went splendidly, and he wanted to take off the makeup as fast as possible and join the audience to enjoy the circus right after, so I volunteered my trailer. I wasn't inside, though I wanted to be. He ran in, washed off the makeup in my trailer's bathroom sink, wiped off the remainder on a towel, and made it inside the Big Top in time for the opening of the show. After the show, I returned to my trailer to find the trashed towel. I preserved it inside a plastic bag, and later that month, we auctioned off this towel at a gala to raise funds for the Big Apple Circus' own traveling school, The One Ring Schoolhouse. Paul signed an affidavit, personally certifying that this was, in fact, the towel he had trashed. With two security guards accompanying me into the ring, I carried "The Newman Towel" inside a briefcase, to which I was handcuffed. The auctioneer read aloud the affidavit and proceeded to jack up the price until the final bid was made. $2,000! Someone in America owns my towel, "The Newman Towel."

People were throwing money so readily at items during that auction that I ran back to my trailer and found some underwear. That raised $200. Somewhere in America, someone owns "The Underwear of Lubin." $2,000 for Paul's towel. $200 for my underwear. Does that mean I am one-tenth as famous as Paul Newman? I would happily take that!

Paul was often backstage after shows and happy to greet the artists and crew, along with his amazing wife, Joanne Woodward. One year, at the end of the show, we were told that he wouldn't be able to come backstage, so we all scattered after that. I was in my trailer taking a shower when my wife Roberta knocked on the door to the bathroom and said, "Honey, Paul Newman and Joanne Woodward are standing outside the trailer." I threw on a towel, still soaking wet and soapy, opened the door of the trailer, and asked, "What do you two want now?" They both laughed (thank GOD) and we posed for photos outside the trailer with me freezing and topless, and wearing a towel. Not pretty, but pretty damn cool.

At the finale of another show, Paul was sitting front row center, and as I took a bow with the entire cast, Paul stood up and hugged me. He commented to me about how the juggler was so good, he could have juggled the books and kept Enron out of bankruptcy. I repeated what Mr. Newman had said to one person and suddenly the next day it was in Cindy Adams' celebrity gossip column in the New York Post and syndicated across the country. That was Paul Newman.

He loved being the auctioneer at his daughter's charity events. I was sent across the plaza to Avery Fisher Hall at Lincoln Center because

Performing at the Circus Festival in Izhevsk Russia 2011, photo by Ann Hageus.

Big Apple Circus donated four ringside seats for the auction and they wanted me there to represent them. Paul was just standing around before the auction began and I walked up to him and told him, "I will donate $100 to your daughter's charity right now if you call my wife on my cell phone." Without hesitation, Paul asked me for my cell, called my wife, and talked to her for five minutes. All I could hear was his end of the conversation, but I could tell she had asked him if it were really Paul Newman, because he'd responded with one of the all-time great lines: "Yes, this is actually Paul Newman, but sometimes I feel like Redford."

When Paul Newman passed away, the world lost one of its great artists, and one of its finest human beings as well. I ran into his daughter, Clea, the following year at her charity event, and I told her how sorry I was about her dad. She thanked me and shared with me that she hadn't yet been able to mourn her dad's passing. The demands on her time had been enormous as she accommodated everyone else's grief over his death. It must have been tough on Clea throughout her life to have such a hugely famous father – and not just famous, but beloved throughout the world.

I'm just happy to have met the man...and that Paul Newman hugged me.

Performing with one of the wonderful audience volunteers at Big Apple Circus, Photo by Andy Bell.

Book Titles My Publisher Turned Down

At the insistence of my friend, Amity Stoddard, a gifted writer, redhead, and fellow movie junkie, I thought I would treat you to some of the brainstorming that went into finding the perfect title for this book. Here are the titles we didn't go with.

Memoirs of a Bitter Transvestite Clown
My Ex-Wife Makes My Dresses
I Pissed Off Meryl Streep
Laughter on Six Incontinence
Grandma: The Man, The Myth, The Legend, The Hack
One Small Step for a Man, One Giant Leap in Elephant Poop
Stay in School Kids or This Could Happen To You
F.A.R.T. - Funny And Really Talented*
My Dress or Yours...
Life is a Circus, Until Tax Season
My Dress is Red, My Eyes are Brown, My Hair is Leaving
Call Me Nancy
Grandma Did NOT Get Run Over by a Reindeer, Sheesh
The Man Who Almost Flunked Out of Clown College
I Live in Sweden, So Naturally I am a Cross Dresser
Oops, That Wasn't My Whoopee Cushion
Laughter: The Best Medicine Besides Lipitor
May All Your Days Be Days Off
Sawdust in My Shorts
Wildebeests of the Savannah
Hyena Hyena
If Someone Says Quit Clowning Around One More Time...
What the Hell is Going on Under That Dress?
Will the Real Grandma Please Stand Up? Oh, You Already Are
How To Raise Normal Children When Dad is a Cross-Dresser
The Old Lady Who Pays Alimony
Transvestites of the American West
I Am From Earth, You Obviously Have Another Story

* Contributor: Danielle LubinJokes and Stories

I did stand-up comedy from 1978 to 1982. I worked at Catch a Rising Star in New York City, The Comedy Store in Los Angeles, and at various clubs in San Diego, Orlando, and Boston. Stand-up comedy is by far the most difficult and painful art form imaginable. Hang around with stand-up comedians and it can get depressing. Most stand-ups are fine and lovely people, though often neurotic like me. I am simply saying it got depressing hanging out in tiny back rooms in smoke-filled clubs for hours waiting to go on. The wait was usually worth it, but not always. You need stage time to get better. By the end of my short-lived stand-up comedy career in New York City in 1982, I'd had a solid ten minutes. That was it… but it was solid. The most I made was $40 in a club in Worcester, Massachusetts. The next time I worked in a stand-up comedy club was thirty-one years later.

My comedy set consisted of me standing there and saying, "Hi, my name is Barry Lubin and I'd like to tell some jokes and stories." Then I would pause and look at the audience and after a while, say, "I really can't tell jokes or stories." I would then proceed to do physical bits, most of which I learned as a circus clown but adapted to the stand-up stage. I would throw popcorn onto my tongue. I would take an LP record cover of Barbra Streisand, spin it on my index finger, use my other index finger like a record needle, and sing Streisand's iconic song, "People." (People / People who need people / Are the luckiest people…) And the record cover would fall off my finger and I would stop. Odd stuff like that.

Cut to February 2013, in Stuttgart, Germany, where I headlined at a stand-up club. I hadn't done stand-up in over three decades, nor was I interested in going back to nightclub work. But, friends with whom I had worked in Hannover, Germany, at a great outdoor festival known as Kleines Fest, told me I had a standing invitation at their club whenever I could make it. In February of 2013, I had a small tour planned, with a gap just at the right time to accept their kind invitation. I signed a contract for 213 euros, plus hotel and travel expenses.

I arrived at the club for rehearsal in the late afternoon. Friends met me there; they were a comedy trio known as Eure Mutter (which translates to "Your Mother"). They are three young and multi-talented guys, and funny as hell. They combine brilliant physical comedy with music and political humor, and are very popular in Germany. Their club is sold out months in advance whenever they are performing. They host the night's festivities, try out some new material (and some old material), and bring up each comedian during the show. When I arrived, they informed

The cast of the Aachen Circus Festival. Photo by Kurt Sikora

me that I was headlining. I had never headlined. When I did stand-up, I opened or middled, which meant I didn't close. The closer spots are occupied by very good people who know how to finish a show with a flourish and provide the highest point of the evening. I have been featured in various theater, circus, and nightclub shows during my forty-year career, but had never headlined.

Headliner? Closer? WHAT? I told them I had never done it, and they found it hard to believe, actually certain that I was kidding. I assured them I was not kidding. They said it would be fine – that the stage and audience were perfect for my talents, and that I was the natural closer to their show. Have I neglected to mention that I was not going to be doing any stand-up comedy in this show? Did I mention I don't speak German and this was Stuttgart? I decided to accept this punishment and try to learn something from it. Oh, did I mention I was going to headline this show as Grandma, wearing full clown makeup, wig, and costume? Yes, a cross-dressing, silent clown headlining at a stand-up comedy club…

I was able to sit at a table designated for the evening's talent and watch the first half of the show. It was interesting to watch people get laughs by telling jokes and stories in German while not understanding a single word, except "Obama," "Lance Armstrong," "Arnold Schwarzenegger," and "marijuana." I watched the rhythm of the joke and the roll of the audience as the speaker delivered the material. It was actually quite fun. At the same time I was asking myself, "What the fuck am I doing headlining a stand-up comedy club in Stuttgart?"

Intermission. I headed backstage, put on my makeup and costume, set my props, and tried to figure out a way not to bomb. Bombing: one of many comedy terms involving death, used in either good or bad ways.

I bombed = I sucked.

I died = I sucked.

I killed = I did really well and they loved me.

I fucking killed = I did really, really well, the audience totally loved me, and I tend to over-exaggerate.

Comedians compliment other comedians with the latter, never the former. You would not hear a fellow comedian say you bombed. You would tell them you bombed, at which point they would say, "Nah, the audience sucked; you were fine." Or if you killed, they might say, "Hey man, you killed tonight." This might be said with envy or awe, or more likely as a statement of fact.

Stand-ups work a little differently than clowns. The audience is occasionally right when you suck, and always right when you kill. It is much worse when you are making a ton of money and the audience sucks; though you may wish to blame the audience, the bottom line is: you bombed.

I have bombed many times. I have killed many times.

Guess which sets you remember most vividly....

I have seen some of my comedy heroes working live and it is a mixture of dying and killing.

I went to see Steve Martin on stage before he was a superstar.

He killed.

I saw Gary Shandling on stage.

He bombed.

For some odd reason, I find it comforting when someone I look up to bombs. It makes me realize that I can be that bad. I never wish on anyone to stink up the stage, but I've been there, done that.

The Clan, starring Marion Legler to my right and her fantastic family, the best fans anyone could hope for!
Photo by Ann Hageus

I once performed for 21,000 people in a circus in Detroit and died show after show, which was painful as hell – partly because I was being paid a boatload of money to perform. I started the weekend poorly, but ended it well. In other words, I had enough shows booked with this circus to try to figure it all out. By the final three shows, I was killing. When you bomb in front of 21,000 people, it just sounds like nothing is happening. When you kill in front of 21,000 people, YOU ARE A ROCK STAR! When that happened, the stars, moon, and earth aligned with my universe. It was a feeling I will never forget – one that I have chased and occasionally captured at other times in my career. The adrenaline rush of that kill instantly made me feel how a rock star

With Bello Nock. Photo by Betrand Guay, Courtesy of Big Apple Circus

must feel. I inadvertently stopped my act at that moment when I got that first huge reaction in the arena. The waves of laughter washed over me, the energy coming at me from both sides of the building, and I stopped. Then I realized what I was doing and proceeded.

Back to Stuttgart. I knew the audience was terrific that night. This was obvious in English, German, silent, whatever. I walked out there and it was kind of crazy. They accepted me because I just allowed myself enough vulnerability, and in a way, I let them know, non-verbally, that I knew being a transvestite clown in full makeup and costume on the stage of a stand-up club was completely absurd. My performance started well, sagged a little in the middle, and ended really well. (THANK GOD!) I did a lot of my usual shtick that I would do in arenas, in theater shows, festivals, on television, and in the circus, and they bought it. I didn't kill, but I would say I did well.

Each time I go out there, I have to make it happen for the audience. That is the pressure and the joy of live entertainment. Sometimes it happens without me being "on." I have to admit that I am "off" quite often, but I try to keep that to myself. I still trot out my material and character and pray that it works. Maybe that is the key: the desire to make it work, regardless of the energy in

With Dick Monday and Tiffany Riley in Big Apple Circus Big Top Doo Wop 2001. Photo by Bertrand Guay, Courtesy of Big Apple Circus

the room or within myself.

People often ask, "What do you do when you aren't in the mood?" They are making the good assumption that clowns are only human. They are right. My answer is this: it is like a plumber being hired to fix your sink. I am the plumber. You called me to fix your sink, and you couldn't care less whether I am in the mood to fix your sink or not. You shouldn't have to care whether my cat died, my girlfriend dumped me, or that I have a head cold. You just want your sink fixed. My job is to use the tools I have at hand and fix your sink, plain and simple. If I do that well, you will be pleased, and you will pay me for my services. Not only that, you might just tell your friends and neighbors that I am pretty good at fixing sinks, so maybe they should call me to provide that service for them one day. That is the bottom line. Performing is the same thing. That is professionalism.

A clown I admire, David Larible, came to a circus in which I was performing; the audience wasn't good, but neither was I. After the show, I complained, as many of us performing artists are wont to do, that he HAD to come to THAT show, of all shows. Naturally, I want my heroes, peers, and those I greatly respect to see me at my best and when the audience is also at their best. His answer to me was beautiful and it taught me a lot. David said he would rather see me under those conditions when the audience and I are not perfect, because it is then that my craft shows. When it is hard, my ability to do a professional performance is at risk, in play, on shaky ground. It is then that my professional skills and abilities and spirit are truly

With Musical Director of Big Apple Circus, Rob Slowik, one of the greatest trumpet players and partners of all time, photo by Paul Gutheil

on display. WOW!

Does it matter what I am being paid, whether there is pressure or not for an engagement? I often say that the free gigs are the hardest. You have given your services for free to a friend, charity, as a favor, and you naturally want to do well. Pay me a ton of money and yes, the pressure is there, but so is the realization that, regardless if I kill or bomb, I will most likely receive my agreed upon fee. Do enough of those well-paid gigs and bomb routinely, and chances are your gigs will start to dry up pretty fast and your reputation will go to hell.
Guess there's always birthday parties...

With my manager and Artistic Director of Big Apple Circus, Guillaume Dufresnoy, photo by Danielle Lubin.

No one is smarter than a dumb person, with exceptions

Pay it Forward

When I came into the business of show in 1974, I was told that the old timers, often affectionately referred to as "dinosaurs," were resentful of the new people coming into clowning by way of Clown College. The dinosaurs had earned their keep with many years of backbreaking work and their experiences were unparalleled. Here we were, upstarts, eager and young and knowing nothing, so understandably they didn't want to share their hard-earned secrets to success with us. The idea I was given was that they wouldn't share much of anything with us. We could learn it the hard way, much like they had over many years. Experience is everything.

What I found out was just the opposite.

As long as I was respectful and listened well, I was offered a wealth of information from all the great sources that surround-

Ringmaster Petit Gougou in Monte Carlo, Photo by Danielle Lubin

ed me at Clown College and on the touring units of "The Greatest Show on Earth." My first mentor, and one with whom I was lucky enough to tour and become friends, was Lou Jacobs. With decades of experience behind him, and no worry about us young whippersnappers stealing his gags or his job, Lou took all of us under his wing, and his wig, and willingly, happily, passed along his treasure trove of knowledge. Those of us lucky enough to be in one of the classes he taught, or lucky enough to have toured with him, will never forget this man. Bigger than life, loved by millions; simple, humble, sweet, and funny as hell.

The list was short of those who mentored me simply, because the business is contracting, not expanding. The dinosaurs were few and far between when I began my career. I have always considered myself a student of the arts, and I listened and learned by watching the likes of Bobby Kaye, Dwayne Thorpe, and Lou Jacobs. My lead instructor in Clown College was a young man named David Nicksay. He was in his mid-twenties, but had a few years of road experience, and he was intuitive, smart, funny, and a great teacher. He later went on to a successful career as a Hollywood producer (having produced Legally Blonde and Pacific Heights, among dozens of others). Many years later, when I was starring in the Big Apple Circus in New York City, David and I met up for coffee. A bus passed by, and on its side was an ad for the circus with a big picture of me. This successful Hollywood producer looked at me and said, "How cool is that!" And I had him to thank in part for setting me on a path to be on the side of a bus. David gave me the energy, inspiration, and information necessary to get where I wanted to go, which at the beginning was an ego-fueled desire to be the best in the world.

Lou Jacobs gave me the most valuable information of all when he told me, and anyone else who would listen, what the secret to comedy was. It went exactly like this: "If they laugh, it's funny. If they don't, it ain't." That was it, folks. Nothing could be truer; now, then, forever. It always left us wanting more, but pure and simple, it gave us full responsibility to make the audience happy. If they weren't happy, we didn't do our job, and if they were, hallelujah!

His favorite expression to describe a clown routine that was a complete mess was to call it "shpaghetti." in a thick German accent. It simply meant it was unclear and impossible to tell what was going on within the clown number. If it's shpaghetti, it isn't good and has about a zero percent chance of getting a laugh. Shpaghetti is similar to a stand-up comic mumbling a joke no one can understand.

When Lou was honored at the historic gathering of the 20th Reunion of Clown College, at its original home at the Venice Arena, he was introduced by the master of ceremonies. As he stood backstage, ready for his entrance into the arena to a worshipful audience of five hundred alumni, we all started to chant, "Lou Lou Lou Lou Louuuuuuu." In the cacophony, Lou actually thought we were booing him and refused to come out. We waited and waited, but one of the other clowns backstage with Lou told him what was actually happening: the chants were "Louuuu," not "boooo." Finally, he walked out to cheers and a standing ovation like I had never seen nor heard before in my life. That was the effect the man had on us all.

When I was teaching at Clown College a few years later, Lou passed away during the opening week, and we were all generously invited by his family to attend his funeral. These new clowns had no idea who Lou really was, personally, but they could certainly understand the contribution the man had made to their art. At the end of the service, I was asked by the family to be a pallbearer. It was one of the greatest honors of my life, and the thing I remember most from that day: that man was heavy! I guess love and talent weigh a lot.

We always wanted to hear stories from the dinosaurs: what it was like back then, what the other clowns did to each other for jokes, the best and worst story from performances over the years, favorite towns, least favorite towns. I am a bit surprised that newcomers don't ask me much when I visit Ringling's clown alley on tour, or perhaps they are afraid to ask.

To them I say: please ask.

My job, the way I view it, is to give back what I have learned. I believe that my experiences, both positive and negative, can be helpful. It's not a matter of going out of my way and asking who would like my information. It is more that I look for opportunities to teach, and hope my teaching skills are good enough to pass along whatever it is that I know. I am getting better at it.

I was so eager to find my place in Sweden that I offered to run a workshop for Clowns Without Borders, a great organization with chapters around the world, and with a very active group based in Sweden. They go to places in need around the world, often the same places as Doctors Without Borders: refugee camps, earthquake- or flood-ravaged areas, poverty-stricken places. I tried my best at this workshop and it was a total flop. It was so bad that I have barely forgiven myself to this day for doing such a bad job. As my failure plodded along, near the end I thought I would be fine once I taught the group one of my specialties: water spitting. They all gamely came outside with me in the dead of winter to try. Just a few moments into what I hoped would save the workshop from disaster, the leader of the group, Nalle Laanela, informed me that in certain cultures, it is taboo to have anything come out of your mouth, water or otherwise. Failure! Failure! Failure!

Oh well.

I was determined never to fail again on so monumental a

David Shiner, Christian Lindeman, Peter Shub, me and Ann Hageus, Festival Der Traume in Innsbruck Austria 2013. (Festival der Traume)

scale. Of course, that very determination nearly guaranteed it would happen again, so perhaps the value of that failure was to realize I could learn from it, and it could motivate me to try and do better. I'm not an educator by trade, even though I am shifting more and more in that direction. I am a clown.

Hotel Clownifornia, with David Shiner, Christian Lindemann, Peter Shub and Ann Hageus. (Festival der Traume)

Ironically, in my chosen trade, I fail quite often, sometimes spectacularly. The lesson always is: the sun rose the next day, and no one died. Why should teaching be any different? And when I teach, I teach failure. (That is something I teach very well.)

I attended Hebrew school (though technically it was Hebrew afterschool) before the magic age of thirteen. It was there that I learned some important lessons about teaching. My teacher, Mr. Hafetz, explained that the most important thing a teacher can do for his class is love them. He also told me that a teacher is often more important in one's life than their parent(s). That is an arguable fact – maybe hopeful on Mr. Hafetz's part – but regardless, the man knew the importance of connecting with students.

What do I know that's valuable to others? I'm not sure. I have more experience than they do, and I have a point of view about what I want my clowning to be, and what my strengths and shortcomings are. I feel somewhat limited that I still have not developed a great deal of my character's possibilities. It's hard to argue with success, but I believe there are more sides to Grandma; pathos, ethos, sympathetic notes I have never played. I always say that I don't want to be caught trying to manipulate an audience's emotions. Red Skelton did it artfully, and while Jerry Lewis did it brilliantly, you could occasionally see his machinations. Never with Red. The art of emotionally ripping someone's guts out in one moment, and in the next moment making them laugh, is an art I admire enormously, but one I haven't even come close to approaching. I wish I had that ability. People say that Grandma does touch them emotionally, but that is a byproduct of me just wanting to make them laugh. It is not my intention.

In Izhevsk, Russia. Me and two Swedish contorionists, the Haglund Sisters. I love my job!!!
Photo by Ann Hageus

I suppose there is something revealing about the person who simply tries to make someone laugh. People read into that and ask about the meaning behind it. The meaning for me is not important. I just go out there and try to get laughs. Period. Spencer Tracy was told he was a great actor, and he responded, "Shhh, don't tell anyone." I believe Mr. Tracy meant that he was trying to give the best, most natural performance possible. The rest was just someone else's opinion.

I often tell people that I'm not interesting. People often misunderstand what I mean when I say I'm not interesting, so I will try to explain. There is so much "new circus" and "new clowning" out there in the world nowadays, and perhaps one could argue that is far more interesting than a little guy in a red dress and gray wig doing headstands on a whoopee cushion.

I am not trying to tell a story, change the world, make a political statement, carry a theme, dig deeply into the emotions of humankind, bare my soul, comment on the human condition, end war and famine, or be thought of as someone with gravitas. I just go out there and try to earn my keep by making you laugh. It is why people hire me. If you want someone interesting, you've got the wrong clown. I'm the clown who lip-syncs to Britney Spears, honks horns, rides a skateboard into a hockey wall, and throws popcorn onto my tongue.

Do people take more away from my performances than my simple desire to make them happy? I know now that they do. It would be naive to act as if I didn't realize that were true. But my intention is simple, and my path to get where I want to go – that is also simple. I want you to have a good time and to escape from your worries and troubles for just a little while.

People have dolls of me, along with bibs, coffee mugs, bobbleheads, and countless photos. I am on people's Christmas cards, on their refrigerators, in their beds. I am so pleased when I hear someone still has an item of mine. The honor touches me deeply. It means the character remains, the feelings of laughter and happiness carried on after we parted, and that perhaps I affected a life or two for a few moments.

So, I'm not interesting. I have nothing much to say. Some may think what I do is overly simplistic, what might be called "low art." Others may read too much into it. I really think this: if you laugh, I did my job, and if you don't, well, I am working on that. Interesting clowns create new worlds. I live in yours.
Interesting clowns have a lot to say. I have only one thing to say: it would be my pleasure and my honor if you take this fun little ride with me, and let's have a few laughs together.

> **Please do not stare when you see a famous person. Use the escalator.**

Sobriety, Elephants, and Losing the Funny

The fantastic Mayor, His Honor, Michael Bloomberg. Photo by Joel Dein

On May 15, 1987, I got sober. Prior to that, I was a functioning alcoholic and pothead. I never missed work and most people never knew I was drunk or high… but I was. I spent what I estimate to be the value of a house or two on marijuana over the years. I even had a dealer in New York who took checks and credit cards. I started using in 1970, a month after arriving for my freshman year at Emerson College. To start off, the drinking age was eighteen at the time, so I was legally allowed to imbibe; then I walked into my three-person dorm room and found a Che Guevara poster on the wall and nine pounds of marijuana in the closet, each pound neatly wrapped in a paper bag. Heavy stuff for a conservative small-town boy…and very alluring. It also scared the hell out of me. This was major illegal stuff, especially in that quantity. For a kid who never even had a traffic ticket at that point in his life, it was frightening.

The only time I had come into contact with illegal substances in my life prior to college was being offered a strange little pipe by a high school friend while we were vacationing in Miami Beach. It was odd to me and I turned it down. It also made me realize there was a lot more going on in my surroundings than of which I was generally aware. I certainly didn't feel left out by that awareness, but I wondered what else was going on – strange, wonderful, terrible stuff just next door.

Through high school, I never drank, except for tiny sips of wine on Jewish holidays. I don't recall wanting more. Then I was on my own in college, with no one telling me how to do my hair, what to wear, or when to go to bed. Free at last! A month after being around bags and bags of pot and clouds of smoke, I finally broke down and tried it.

I loved it.

Like all the other potheads I was with, my perception of

marijuana was that it was safe, non-addictive, cheap, and fun...at least at first.

In my sophomore year at Emerson, I got a job at a nearby bar, the Bull and Finch Pub. The outside of the Bull and Finch is what you see on the television show, Cheers. (Ironically, years later, I served as a technical advisor on one episode of that show.) At the Bull and Finch, I was the bus boy and worked in the freezing basement most of the time. Every twenty minutes or so, I brought a bus tray upstairs to the bar, cleared drinks and bottles, and took them back down to the basement to wash them. It was an easy job, no thinking involved, and the money was amazingly good. I soon found out why the pay was so high: the basement was infested with rats, and not just your garden-variety rats, but rats the size of a Volkswagen. It scared the crap out of me when they skittered around and ran into my ankles while I was washing glasses, but I needed the money. So, I found a solution. Just outside of the kitchen was a giant refrigerator containing tons of imported beers. When my shift began, I took eight bottles of fine beer, chugged them quickly before the manager could catch me, and suddenly the rats didn't matter in the least. In retrospect, I don't understand how I managed to not act drunk when doing my job, but I never remember being perceived that way at all by patrons or the nice people who I worked with. Maybe the rats knew. I also don't recall feeling drunk. I felt numb. Numb was the goal, and it became my mantra throughout my using days.

After a few weeks of this, on a day off from work, I noticed I was yearning for a beer.

No, I needed a beer.

I had to have a beer.

That scared the hell out of me. Was I becoming alcohol dependent? I decided at that moment to stop drinking so much. The easy solution? I increased my pot smoking! I thought it was a good drug – not dangerous, not bad like

With Meryl Streep at Lincoln Center at the Mayor's Arts and Culture Awards, 2010, photo by Joel Dein. Photo by Joel Dein

alcohol, quite benign. In time, I became a genuine pothead. I was using it daily, but maintaining my grades, never missing a shift at work, and keeping my head above water. I didn't realize then that my ever-increasing pot smoking was bringing me down in nearly every way possible, and even threatening my existence. As my need for drugs grew, I laughed at my dear friend, comedian D.F. Sweedler, who was one of my college roommates. He never drank, nor smoked pot, nor snorted cocaine, nor dropped acid. At the time I just couldn't understand that. Now I admire him enormously for it.

My first experience with cocaine was the classic "first one is free" offer by a dealer I met just outside the Emerson Student Union. It was considered, at the time, a non-addictive drug – especially by my dealer. Of course, he'd say anything to sell a few grams. I used cocaine often during my twenties. It was fun, and the only disadvantages were my lack of serious money and how crappy I felt coming down. The highs never lasted very long, and I was never rich enough to have a steady supply on hand. Occasionally, I even performed under the influence. When I was doing cocaine in New York City, a friend told me that he was relatively sure I was actually snorting heroin. Incredulous, I asked why that would be so. He told me that the price of heroin had dropped in New York City because a huge supply had been dumped on the market, and since there was so much out there, it was cheaper than coke. He reasoned that dealers were probably substituting heroin, and I freaked out and never did cocaine again. I had my limits, and that scared me straight. Not into sobriety, just off cocaine.

I tried "angel dust" a few times, which is apparently a horse tranquilizer. I never felt tranquil under the influence, though – just hyped up and very angry – and I recall clenching my teeth for hours at a time. That experiment lasted just a short time. I then used marijuana soaked in opium a few times, not realizing how dangerous that might be. It was all about the high, and searching for a better one, and this was a helluva good high, but too expensive to continue.

My LSD use was short-lived. I remember, in a hazy sort of way, dropping acid about five times, with the last time being alone. It was my only bad trip and it scared me really badly. My first trip was with a good friend from Emerson. We visited his home in Vermont in the fall, at the time when leaves were changing and at their richest color. It was exquisite and beautiful…until my friend was hanging horizontally under a big limb of a tree and it snapped. He crashed to the ground with the limb slamming on top of him. I remember him lying there and I kept saying, for no reason at all, "You're okay. You're okay." I must have thought saying that would make it so, as the drug had paralyzed me from doing anything useful, like helping him. Thankfully, he lived. I remember another time tripping with friends in Boston and looking up at the night sky and observing that the clouds would move across the sky, then back up quickly, then move again. Over and over I observed this. Another time I listened to Stan Getz, the great jazz saxophonist, and realized he was one of the greatest jazz musicians of our time. Well, Stan Getz was one of the greatest, but the realization in that moment felt like I discovered fire. It was so profound. And then for my last trip, which I did alone, I was in a nightmare that I couldn't escape. I stopped people on the streets of Boston just to ask them to talk me down, and after several blew me off, one kindly hung out with me for hours until I was relatively sane again. (I have no idea why, but sometimes the kindness of strangers is incalculable.) It scared me so badly that I never dropped acid again. It was mind-altering, and at first, mind-expanding. LSD caused me to appreciate the tiniest things in the world, which were usually uninteresting to me. Oddly enough, with age and life experience, I now appreciate those things without the use of drugs.

I was into Quaaludes for a little while. I had difficulty functioning under the influence of downers, but I liked the feeling. I experimented with different doses, none of which allowed me to function. My last experience with Quaaludes was in a fraternity house at the University of Pennsylvania where a friend of mine was living. I had one tablet, found myself lying on the floor about two inches from the cat pee on the carpet, unable to move for twelve hours. How that is enjoyable, I have no clue.

On the long trips between cities, while I was with the Ringling show, I started doing amphetamines. The pills allowed me to stay up during the train runs and watch America go by, mostly alone. I abused amphetamines, but never at work, the same as Quaaludes. I knew I wouldn't be able to function during a performance under the influence of the uppers and downers, though I could manage while off work. These pills were readily available and I am sure they still are. The feeling I hated the most was coming down off amphetamines, as it was nearly always an out-of-control depression. At those times I smoked a joint to ease the transition. I was medicating myself so I could handle the effects of other medications. It made sense to me at the time.

    I finally pushed the boundaries and did the dumbest thing a clown could possibly do. I decided to smoke some pot with a buddy during the fifteen-minute intermission of the Ringling show. We sneaked out of the arena in Jacksonville, found a good hiding place, and shared a very potent joint. Twenty minutes later, when the THC was kicking in full force, it was time for me to climb on top of my elephant, Tichi, and be part of the big elephant production number, which consisted of eighteen elephants with clowns and dancers on top, plus the rest of the circus cast dancing on the arena floor. The first thing you learn when you ride an elephant is that the most comfortable position is a little ways back behind the neck. You hold on with your inner thigh muscles and it is really fun. There is a harness around the elephant's neck to hold onto when they sit up, but as they run, it is best to sit back and lean at the turns. I was lifted up onto Tichi by having her handler ask her to lift her leg. This action would fling me up and on top of the elephant. That was always a helluva lot of fun…when sober. Once on top, I had a sudden realization that I was high as a kite, and it scared the hell out of me. The first thing the elephants did in their number was run fast into the arena and step up onto silver metal elephant tubs, which were about three feet high, and await the first command. Scared to death, I sat way up on the neck, holding onto the harness for dear life as Tichi took off. The ride was ridiculously bumpy for me, but there was no way I was going to let go of the harness that time. Tichi stepped up onto her elephant tub, which was located at one end of the hippodrome track, and I had a sudden realization that thousands of people were looking at me, but for some reason I couldn't understand why. Then I reminded myself that I was a clown in a circus and I was sitting on top of a two-and-a-half-ton elephant…which made me panic even more. I couldn't breathe. I thought I was going to jump off Tichi and run, but then I thought that if I jumped off at the moment the trainer gave the command to Tichi to do the first trick – a simple slow turn on top of the elephant tub – I'd be squished like a grape. Plus, it was a helluva long way down, so I hung on for dear life. Amazingly, I lived.

A normal person wouldn't do that ever again.

The second dumbest thing a clown could possibly do is to ride an elephant while stoned a few hundred times more. For some moronic reason, I kept doing it. I was a dumb clown. Fortunately, I was never busted for RUI: Riding Under the Influence. As stupid as it was, I think I did it for the thrill – a way to push my limits…and who knows, maybe I had a bit of a death wish. What a daredevil I was then!

With Chris Meloni, star for many years of Law and Order, SVU, photo by Danielle Lubin. Photo by Danielle Lubin

There were days during my using when I would be on tour, leaving my wife and baby at home, and I would go out in desperate search for a joint. I remember riding around in our pick-up truck in some very questionable places asking almost anyone if they knew where I could score some pot. I often hear that marijuana is not addictive, but I certainly had, at the least, a psychological addiction going. I was driving around, risking my life and the safety of my family, in search of a high. I felt horribly guilty, very afraid, and at the same time I felt like it was an absolute necessity that I get high. Most of the time, I was able to score something. It was an impulse I couldn't resist – didn't want to resist, either. Escape was not an option – it was the only thing. Those memories are seared in my brain.

When my first child, Danielle, was born, and my guilt over my excessive pot smoking grew and grew, the money I was spending on my so-called benign habit was increasing, too. I was no longer able to

With the fabulous Isabella Rossellini. Photo by Emily Lubin

A day at Kleinesfest in Hanover Germany where I was not feeling so great, photo by Ann Hageus

smoke regular pot. It just didn't work for me anymore. I was buying primo. I felt my life spiraling out of control and downward, and I was very unhappy. Not only did I feel terrible, but I also felt hopeless. And then a dear friend of mine, Peter – someone whom I had gotten into pot smoking years before, ironically – talked to me about getting sober. I was so miserable, but also very lucky that I listened to him, and a short while later I got into a twelve-step program. Though the beginning of my sober life wasn't perfect, on May 15, 1987, I had my last mind-altering substance – an imported beer – and I have been sober since, thanks to the grace of God and the help of a lot of fellow alcoholics. I remember having that last beer quite clearly, and the idea that it would be my last one didn't appeal to me very much then, but I was resigned to getting sober…and I did.

For the first nine months of my sobriety, I was no longer funny and I truly thought that my humor wouldn't come back. I thought that pot was the only thing that made me funny. I listened to story after story in twelve-step program meetings about recovery, and I told my own story. Because marijuana was my last drug of choice, I joined Marijuana Anonymous, known as MA, which was very new then, and I fit right in with lots of newly sober people. We were different – special – because our drug wasn't the hard stuff, though it still affected our lives. However, I quickly realized that since it was a new program, no one had long-term sobriety. Hell, I was thought of as a kind of Zen master of sobriety for my nine months of clean living, because no one else had that much time behind them. I knew I needed to be in Alcoholics Anonymous, where there were people with much more sobriety, wisdom, and experience to learn from. While I kept going to MA, Alcoholics Anonymous became my lifesaver.

As of this writing, I have not had one drink, toke, snort, or pill for twenty-seven years. I did have two experiences that scared the hell out of me, though. One time on an airplane I asked for club soda and was served vermouth. I took a big chug before realizing what I had done and freaked out. The flight attendant started to cry because of what she had done, but I assured her that it was not going to cost the woman her job, nor my sobriety. I hadn't chosen to drink. The other time, I was performing in high temperatures in a circus parade in Milwaukee when I had lain down in the middle of the street to rest and to hopefully make the crowd laugh. A woman came over with a water bottle and I invited her to spill it down my throat. It was not water, but some form of alcohol. I freaked out, spit it out to the delight of the audience, and quickly left. I am not sure if I ingested any, but again I hadn't chosen to drink alcohol.

Today, I am funny, I have a great family, I am in love, I have been blessed with a fantastic career that keeps evolving, and I have achieved far more while sober than I ever did under the influence. I rarely talk about my sobriety publicly. I think there is a risk that people may not understand the disease, and I respect that. I remember hearing from a member of AA, who had many years of sobriety, that he would never lend a dollar to anyone with less than five years of sobriety. That confused me at the time, but so many people bounce in and out of the program that it makes sense to me now. Being sober this long, I understand so much more. The most important thing I now understand is how little I truly understand in this world. It is a great relief, frankly.

I go to work sober, I go to movies sober, I eat sober. Though the idea of doing any of those things without being under the influence of some mind-altering substance seemed un-fun back then, I no longer feel I need it in order to enjoy any as-

Performing on the MV Explorer, photo by Jer Kong.

One of my favorite photos with my partner Ann taken at our theater debut in Stockholm at Teater Galeasen 2011. Photo by Cristofer Grimas

pect of my life. Maybe more importantly, I can get through the worst times without it. It was so easy to escape my problems with pot or other drugs, or alcohol. They were just a way to avoid things. I have nothing else to lean on except my spiritual life. That has kept me going for a long time, along with the influence of so many other sober people, and the knowledge of something I learned: you are never alone. When I am touring, and with the Internet, I can find a meeting anytime, and anywhere I go.

Before every show performance, I say a prayer – something my friend, Ellen, taught me to do. Ellen suggested I make up something, which suits me well, and so I did. I more or less pray for humility to just do the job and not turn it into my own personal ego trip; gratitude for what I have, which is my family, friends, and the people by whom I am lucky enough to be employed; and to go in faith and have fun. Amen. It centers me, gives me the ability to deal with whatever comes my way each show and each day, and it just feels right.

I know that part of the reason for my drug and alcohol use and abuse was to escape from uncomfortable feelings. I was terribly insecure; often afraid of life itself, people, and social circumstances. Using made me forget all those things. What started as recreational use was soon replaced with obsession. I most certainly have an obsessive-compulsive personality, which I have worked on quite a bit. With a combination of readily available drugs and enough money, along with a desire to fit in, it got out of hand pretty fast.

My only drug of choice these days is coffee. I have to watch my coffee use, too, because if I am under the influence of too much caffeine, it actually throws off my timing when I am performing, and it keeps me awake until the wee hours of the morning every so often.

I can hang out in bars and at parties where people are drinking, but it becomes boring after a while if too many people are tipsy.

I cannot be around marijuana smoke. That is a dangerous place for me. I have no desire to drink or use again, but I am smart enough to know that all of those things are right around the corner, next door, and there are plenty of people I know who could acquire it for me easily. If I have one joint, I have come to believe – to know – that it will lead me back to the place where I had no life. If I drink one beer or one glass of wine, it will be the start of a dangerous downward spiral. If I drop acid, or take other mind-altering substances, it will be like falling down the well.
I do not want to fall down the well again.
I will never forget what one alcoholic shared in a meeting in New York. James said, "My first job is to stay sober. My second job is to blow shit out of proportion." It applies to me perfectly.

Celebrities I Have Pissed Off

Because I am a clown, I have met various luminaries from the worlds of entertainment, sports, publishing, business, politics, and royalty. In doing so, I have also managed to piss off a surprising number of them. Let me be clear about one thing, though. As a good friend once pointed out, my ability to irritate others hasn't been limited to just famous folk. That being said, my first encounter with a celebrity was with one of my all-time idols, Gene Kelly. He was hosting a television show in 1975, Highlights of Ringling Brothers and Barnum & Bailey Circus, which was taped for broadcast in the first town in which we toured, just prior to the official March opening at Madison Square Garden. Mr. Kelly was seated with Irvin Feld, the owner and producer of Ringling, and was watching the show he would soon be hosting, narrating, and performing for NBC cameras.

Irvin Feld's longtime assistant, Arnold Bramoff, told me to go over to Gene Kelly

Riding the Macy's Thanksgiving Day Parade route, 2011, Photo by Derrick Blevins.

and sit in his lap. I was just in the second week of my professional career and I took this as a command, more or less. I went over to him and sat on his lap. His facial expression clearly told me that he was extremely unhappy with this invasion of his space. He said nothing, just glared at me. I got up and slowly walked away, feeling quite terrible that I had pissed off Gene Kelly. On the other hand, I can honestly say: I sat in Gene Kelly's lap.

I did a few memorable performances at Lincoln Center's Alice Tully Hall in New York City, during what is called The Mayor's Arts and Culture Awards. Former Mayor Michael Bloomberg himself requested me three times. His Honor hosted it annually, along with a different celebrity each year. I was fortunate enough to be part of these shows honoring arts organizations and artists who have contributed to the culture of New York City. And I have managed to piss off two celebrities during those three years.

Robin Williams with me on the left. Photo by Rob Libbon.

Not a bad percentage.

In the second year, Meryl Streep was co-host. She was designated by the head writer of the event to play straight man/woman to the mayor and me as we did a popcorn routine together. Mayor Bloomberg and I have a few things in common, one of which is a great love for popcorn. Backstage, before the show, I saw that Ms. Streep had entered her dressing room alone and was sitting there with the door open. I asked my friend, Joel Dein, who was acting as my representative from the Big Apple Circus, to go over with me and just say hello. I was not fully dressed at the time; I was essentially in my clown underwear. That didn't piss off Meryl Streep. As we chatted, Ms. Streep told us that she was doing research on a role, for which she would eventually win her a third Oscar: the role of Margaret Thatcher in The Iron Lady. She was very friendly and we chatted for several minutes. She explained to us that during her research into Margaret Thatcher's life, she discovered that she had an odd hobby of collecting pins. I asked Ms. Streep, thinking I was being quite clever, "Is that as deep as you went in researching the character?" She paused and looked at me as if I were a total idiot, which I was, and said slowly, "No, that isn't as deep as I went." I have a feeling, as she accepted her Academy Award in Los Angeles a year later, she thought of that stupid clown who mocked her research.

During the third year, Alec Baldwin was the co-host. I didn't piss off Alec Baldwin at all. I didn't try to, either. Steven Sondheim, well, that is another story. He was the big honoree of the evening, a native New Yorker and the prolific writer of many hits, including, ironically, "Send in the Clowns." Just before Mr. Sondheim was to be introduced and honored for his artistic contributions to the culture of New York City, I was asked by the producer to do a tiny bit. The writer suggested they play the intro to the Broadway version of "Send in the Clowns," and that I come out as if I were to sing dramatically to the sold-out house, only to get yanked off the stage. I pleaded with the writer to let me lip-sync just the first line, and he agreed. When I heard the intro, I walked out dramatically onto the stage, in full Grandma regalia, and with great gravitas, I "sang" the iconic first line as if it were one of the biggest nights of my career on the New York stage. Ironically, it was one of the biggest nights of my career on the New York stage. I have rarely been on any New York stages (though I did play one time each on Broadway, and at Carnegie Hall and Radio City Music Hall). I passionately lip-synced that famous first line, "Isn't it rich, are we a pair?" At that point, Alec Baldwin and the mayor cut me off, and I left the stage, tail between my legs as written, to great laughter and applause. After the show, when I was on stage near Mr. Sondheim, I congratulated him on his honor and asked if I could have a photograph with him. He totally blew me off, didn't have time for me, even though he had time for absolutely everyone else that evening. He walked away, making sure we were never together in any frame of any camera. I must have pissed him off pretty bad, but at least I can honestly say I pissed off Stephen Sondheim. I am

Ringmistress Becky Kimes in Maine. Photo by Emily Lubin

just not sure why.

At the same event, actress and singer Patty LuPone was backstage and I said hello to her, startling her. She told me she thought I was a real woman. I'm afraid I cannot claim I pissed her off, but I can honestly say I startled Patty LuPone, and that I could pass for a real woman.

I totally pissed off Ringo Starr.

I was working at The Forum in Inglewood, California – the former arena that housed the Los Angeles Lakers and lots of other events, including the Ringling Circus. We had all heard that Ringo and his wife at the time, Barbara Bach, were in the audience. During intermission, as I always did, I went into the audience and I just "happened" to find myself within a few feet of Ringo. (Totally on purpose.) A small child had a circus program and sweetly asked me for my autograph. I had no pen, so I leaned over and asked Ringo if he had a pen I could borrow so I could sign MY autograph. He looked at me as if I had just pissed him off...because I had just pissed him off. And now I can honestly say: Ringo Starr didn't give me a pen.

I was lucky enough to meet Bruce Springsteen. He was the honorary chairperson of a hospital charity, and the event was held annually to entertain children who were still ill, or who had successfully recovered from a previous illness or injury at that hospital. I was asked to perform as a representative of the Big Apple Circus, with one of the attractions being the possibility of meeting The Boss. When the chance came, of course I said yes. I shook Mr. Springsteen's hand, and as a joke I told him, "You better wash that hand." He looked pissed off. Worse than that, he was still standing in front of me with no one else around, but he obviously wanted nothing to do with this transvestite clown. I felt really embarrassed. I think he may have actually washed his hand immediately after, because I didn't see him again at the

Just before the start of the Macy's Parade. Photo by Phil Thurston

rather small party.

I met the U.S. Ambassador to the Vatican in the summer of 2010 when he visited Semester at Sea's floating campus as it reached Rome on a twelve-country voyage. I was invited to join a small party to listen to the Ambassador talk about his career before being appointed by President Obama, and what it was like to work with the unique entity known as the Vatican. He was a soft-spoken and very thoughtful and deliberate speaker. After a thirty-minute speech and our applause, we had the opportunity to ask questions. Mine was, "So, do you hang with the Pope?" The U.S. Ambassador looked down, saying nothing. After an uncomfortably long pause, during which he seemed to be collecting himself, he replied, "No, I don't HANG with the Pope." I felt like a complete idiot, which is perhaps a step up from an incomplete idiot, and he avoided me the rest of the afternoon quite effectively.

It says Grandma's Back, but I assure you, the photo is my front

Robert De Niro is a different story. Kinda. I was working with the Big Apple Circus and Mr. De Niro was a friend of the flying trapeze artists, the Flying Gaonas. At one performance, he was sitting in the front row at ringside, and the ringmaster, not realizing it was Robert De Niro, picked him from the audience to participate in a clown number. He is one of my all-time heroes, and no matter who Paul Binder picked from the audience, my job was to place a ridiculous shower cap on that person's head. I was appalled, but I figured I had no choice at that moment. I walked over to Mr. De Niro and placed it on his head and whispered, "I am so sorry." He said, "It's okay," in a resigned sort of way, and he was a good sport about it, doing whatever we asked him to do in our clown number. He didn't come back to the show for 10 years. Years later, I gave that shower cap to a big De Niro fan, who treated the gift like it was one of the actor's Academy Awards.

Philippe Petit was famous for walking a wire impossibly strung between the Twin Towers of the World Trade Center. He had the entire city of New York holding its collective breath as he defied logic and gravity for his amazing feat, and it landed Phillippe a two-year contract with Ringling's Greatest Show on Earth on the same unit as me. I became friendly with Philippe and he gladly shared his wisdom as an original street artist and world conqueror, and he also showed me many of his cool juggling tricks between shows. At that time, I was doing a very unoriginal bit with a peacock feather, which, unbeknownst to me, was considered bad luck in the circus. It's a complicated story – something to do with gypsies and the circle on the feather being an "evil eye" – but regardless, they are not to be used in the circus.

I did not know this.

Between shows, Philippe watched me practice with the peacock feather, and he came over and generously showed me a few little tricks. If he knew about the superstition, he ignored it.

A short while later, as he was doing his act on the high wire, he fell forty-five feet to the ground. The clowns were backstage when the dreaded 12th Street Rag played. That song was not in the usual repertoire of the performance. It was used only in emergencies if someone was hurt, or there was a technical glitch, which stopped the show. When that song came on, all the clowns grabbed a prop with which to improvise and ran out into the arena, hopeful that nothing serious had happened. My heart sunk to see my amazing new friend lying there, not knowing if he was alive or dead. We had to work our hardest to distract the audience while Phillippe was administered aid by paramedics and other circus personnel.

It was the first time he had fallen in his entire career. I felt partly responsible for his misfortune, but Philippe never blamed me. He returned to the circus several months later, after recovering from numerous broken ribs. The memory from that day still makes me cringe. And while he might not have been pissed off, I was pissed at myself for playing with that stupid feather. Superstition or not, I never brought a peacock feather into the ring again.

I worked at Atlantic City's landmark, Steel Pier, from my early to late teens doing various jobs; selling pizza, snow cones, popcorn, soda; and filling candy machines on the amusement pier. One night, as I was enjoying a break, I found a metal ladder way out at the end of the pier and decided to throw it into the ocean, just to see the splash. The next day, the Steel Pier experienced a power failure. There was a cool ride in an actual "diving bell," which went from the deck of the pier all the way to the bottom of the ocean, where one could look out the portholes, and then to everyone's thrill and screams, it returned to the surface of the ocean at high speed. Then it was pulled up to the deck of the pier by an electric pulley system. The bell was designed to float up to the surface of the ocean in an emergency, such as a power failure.

There is a hatch on the top of the diving bell to transport fresh air and to provide an emergency escape via specially designed metal ladder for the ten or so passengers on board. The safety personnel reported that the emergency ladder specifically built for this purpose was nowhere to be found. That meant that the passengers inside had risen to the surface, but were stuck bobbing up and down inside the hot, humid diving bell. The fire department was called and possible solutions were discussed for two hours. The electricity finally came back on and the diving bell rose to the level of Steel Pier's deck. I watched as ten patrons were led off, not feeling too happy, or very well. In an unusual move for me back then, I admitted what I had done the following day. The reactions to my actions were not pretty. Let's just say I never threw anything larger than a stone into the ocean again.

Former Mayor Michael Bloomberg has been very kind to me over the years. He was on the Board of Directors of the Big Apple Circus and was generous with his time and resources. He was running for re-election, and I appeared with him briefly during an event. He was asked publicly if he would like Grandma to help with his re-election campaign. Bloomberg replied, away from the microphone, "No thanks, I want to win." I didn't piss off Mayor Bloomberg, but

Celebrate cover. Courtesy of Big Apple Circus.

DooWop cover. Courtesy of Big Apple Circus.

the interviewer did.

Former New York City Mayor Rudolph Giuliani was scheduled to appear with Big Apple Circus founder, Paul Binder, and me at a press conference at City Hall to honor the many years of service the Big Apple Circus had performed in the New York area. The mayor's advance team told us not to embarrass him by putting a rubber nose on him, or squirting water near/at him, or placing a funny hat on him. Paul and I naturally agreed that we would never do that to the mayor, anyway. The time came for the press conference, and just before it started, we were sternly warned again not to embarrass the mayor. We entered the pressroom and warmly greeted the mayor while a press photographer immediately placed a rubber nose on the mayor and told him to smile. Like a real pro, the mayor didn't blink and posed without commenting on the indiscretion of the photographer. Paul and I both felt really badly for the mayor, but at least we didn't do anything wrong. I can honestly say I didn't piss off Mayor Giuliani, but the photographer did.

James Gandolfini of The Sopranos fame passed away in 2013. I felt sad, partly because I had pissed him off once. When I licensed my character on Big Apple Circus, I had to put the "other Grandma" into the circus at some point, which was usually an 11:00 a.m. matinee. Who should come to that one show in New York but Tony Soprano himself, James Gandolfini. Our P.R. people wanted to get a photo with Mr. Gandolfini and me in hopes of getting it in the newspapers. So, the "other Grandma" performed the first half as I took notes from the audience. Then I hurriedly changed into Grandma and came out to meet him with a photographer during intermission. I introduced myself, and as we had a few shots taken, he said to me, "So I have heard about this

Grandma for years and I finally come to see you and it isn't you!" I apologized profusely, explained the situation, told him that I was a big fan, and he was actually quite nice. We chatted about The Sopranos and his latest film work, and he couldn't have been more generous with his time. Intermission ended, and though I considered performing the second half of the show for him, I didn't want to do that to the other performer. I was really disappointed by the timing, but thrilled to meet someone whom I admired so much.

Ah, show biz...

Grandma Goes To Hollywood cover. Courtesy of Big Apple Circus.

Need I mention the celebrities who have managed to piss me off? There is a list...

Dustin Hoffman pissed me off. Yes, Dustin Hoffman, whom I had always admired and of whose supreme talent I continue to be in awe. After the release of Tootsie, where he played a cross-dresser with incredible finesse and comic genius, we met at the Big Apple Circus. He indicated to me that I must have been inspired by his performance. That pissed me off because Grandma debuted on January 1, 1975, and Tootsie hit the theaters on December 1, 1982. I should sue!

I should probably mention the actress, Ellen Barkin. She didn't piss me off at all. She came backstage after enjoying the Big Apple Circus. Years ago, when the circus had elephants, they often brought one back so celebs could sit on top for a photograph, because those photos often made national publications. Ellen, whom I considered to be one of the sexiest actresses on earth, told our publicist, "I'm not getting up on that thing." Since I was standing next to her, I said, "Well, get on me." She got on, piggyback-style, and the paparazzi shot several photographs. Not one photo even made the local papers. THAT pissed me off, but it sure was fun.

When I was young, I woke up early one morning because

Richard Nixon, then President of the United States, was coming to my hometown of Atlantic City, and I wanted to see him. I waited in a really great spot where I was sure to see him – not because I loved Richard Nixon, but because I was a kid and he was the president. After several hours at the front of a big crowd of people, Mr. Nixon arrived. The paparazzi swarmed in front of me, blocked my view, and I saw absolutely nothing. The next day in the local newspaper there was a big photo of Mr. Nixon, and I could also see myself in the shot. THAT pissed me off.

Am I allowed to talk about celebrities whom I've neither pissed off, nor were pissed off by me? I love Isabella Rossellini. She was generous with her time whenever she came to the Big Apple Circus. She was always very sweet, very unaffected by her fame, and so obviously a very smart person. It always thrilled me to see her, though I always tried to not show it; I didn't want to scare her off. She came to the Big Apple Circus almost every year, and often came backstage after the show whenever she had the time. One year, she threw a little party the day before Christmas in a special area inside the Big Top at Lincoln Center, and she invited me to attend. She gave me a beautiful present: a huge basket filled with her own brand of lotions, shampoos, soaps, perfumes, and moisturizers. She told me, "I know you are a man, but I always think of you as a woman, so I want you to have these gifts." I was touched, even though there was absolutely nothing in the basket for I could use.

Grandma doesn't moisturize. My daughters enjoyed Isabella's generous gifts for quite some time after that party.

Chris Meloni is the former star of Law and Order: SVU, and an amazing talent. A great friend of mine, Judy Weisman, loved that show and was dying for any opportunity to meet him and his co-star, Mariska Hargitay, who often came to the Big Ap-

Play On cover. Courtesy of Big Apple Circus.

ple Circus. One afternoon show, Chris showed up with his lovely wife, Sherman Williams, and I said hello and told him about my friend, Judy. I asked if he could just say hello to her over my cell phone. He didn't hesitate. I called Judy and handed over my phone to Chris. He talked with Judy as she drove on the Massachusetts Turnpike. She was thrilled to death! It was a thrill for me to bring such a big moment to her.

Dance On cover. Courtesy of Big Apple Circus.

During my debut on the Broadway stage, Chris dipped me and kissed me on the lips. Okay, it was a charity event in a Broadway theater on a dark night (meaning there was no show that night) and I was just a tiny part of it. As we exited the stage, we both agreed that he kissed me a bit too long. At a nightclub in New York where I was asked to perform, Chris danced with me and put his hand on my ass, which is one of my secrets of the clown number I do to Natalie and Nat King Cole's "Unforgettable." I always whisper to the man I am dancing with, "Put your hand on my ass, it will get a big laugh." 99% of the time they do, and it does. He did, it did. I can honestly say, Chris Meloni had his hand on my ass and kissed me.

When you buy a big ticket item, make sure it is small.

Being in "The Zone"

There are times in my career where I feel like the universe is in control and I am just a conduit for some inexplicable energy. I have heard it described by others, in writing and in person, with each giving it their own name. I call it "The Zone." There is a flow which I have a hard time describing. I can't force it; it happens rarely, and I am completely cognizant of while it is happening. I have tried to put myself into a position for it to happen again, but that effort never pays off. The energy is sublime when I feel the presence of The Zone. It is like the purring of a very efficient engine, but without the pollution.

Does The Zone have anything to do with inspiration? That fleeting and unreliable energy for which I always hope, but which rarely arrives? Are they even in the same ballpark? I will tell you now: I am unsure of the answer. I just know that I would choose to be inspired all the time, if that were somehow possible; when working, writing, creating, I would hope to find myself both inspired and in The Zone.

When I am in The Zone as a performer, I can feel that things are flowing – that the universe, and the audience and me, are pretty much one and the same. It isn't that I can do no wrong… wrong just isn't in the equation. Flow is. When I am in The Zone as a writer, things seem to write themselves, as if I have tapped into an energy unlike any other. I can hear a particular song and have a

Slappin' on the makeup, Aachen Germany 2012, photo by Kurt Sikora.

Eureka! moment, or an idea pops into my head and the keys start flying beneath my fingers on the laptop. I want to be able to replicate these moments of creative energy, but have never been able to do so by willing it into existence.

Basketball players have described the feeling that the basket was perceptually much bigger and making shots came much easier during that limited time. Baseball players have said that the ball coming from the pitcher looked bigger. Comedians have said that certain things not necessarily funny were getting laughs. For me, it feels like a connection to something more than just the audience. More like I am connected to an indescribable energy. So how do I describe it?

The Zone often happens while flying on airplanes, for some reason. Though I am not a writer per se, I will write a new physical comedy piece, or start a script. I even started writing these memoirs at 35,000 feet. I can write prolifically once airborne. Why is that?

In 2008, when I had to leave the Big Apple Circus for my thyroid cancer operation, Matthew Pauli stepped into the role of Grandma – a job he did incredibly well for six seasons when I was not doing the circus tour in spring and summertime. Mark Gindick, who is a super-talented clown, actor, dancer, and person, was my partner that year in the circus. Ironically, Mark had also played Grandma more than occasionally, but not in this production. Mark and I created a piece that was not working well at all, so he and Matthew had to work with it during the time I was gone. They were unable to do very much to make it work better, though they tried. Mark and I had wanted to change it, and quickly, because it wasn't funny. I had my surgery, and then, as I was recovering, Mark and I went into re-write mode, which took place entirely over the phone as I recovered in New Jersey and Mark performed in Virginia with Matthew. The Zone comes in many forms, and together, Mark and I choreographed, costumed, prop-shopped, and edited the new idea we had, which was simple: Mark channeling Gene Kelly from the iconic movie song and dance number, "Singin' in the Rain," while I provided the "rain." In other words, we created various ways to get Mark wet during this dance and lip-sync number.

I recovered quickly enough to make Lincoln Center brush-up rehearsals just before opening in New York, though I wasn't feeling great, and we threw it together in no time. We were able to accomplish that because we think alike, and he and I both knew that we had to get it done quickly. We put it to lights and music, and the creative team gave us the green light. The following night, we performed it in front of a live audience, and it was a big hit. It was a season long success, in fact.

The Zone!

I was hyper-aware of being in The Zone as I recently performed for an entire weeklong engagement in a hockey arena in New Jersey with Royal Hanneford Circus. At the time, I felt like I shouldn't think about it nor analyze it too closely, or it might pop like a balloon. Though one might call it superstitious, I know The Zone is always fleeting, but I had a feeling it was going to be there during each of the eight shows. In retrospect, that sounds like an unlikely place for The Zone to even have a chance to exist. The atmosphere and venue weren't perfect, but that didn't matter. I went to work each show feeling lighter than air, with my feet barely touching the ground. Invincible is how I felt.

I have felt myself going in and out of The Zone during a show, especially one with multiple appearances. Being off stage can have a cooling effect to a hot performance, and I have been sure that I was still in The Zone prior to making my next appearance in the show and been 100% wrong. Fortunately, I have enough experience to turn in a performance of some sort, regardless. I have found that I cannot just keep it at that level, even if I try, as I am sure The Zone would tell you (if it could speak). The Zone has a life of its own.

"The Un-Zone" also exists, and that unfortunate state of mind is perhaps more easily defined than The Zone. At those times, it feels like I am pushing a truck uphill. Though what I do is just physical comedy, the work can still feel totally hopeless at times. It is at those moments when I hope my experience will allow me to have the grace to turn in a good performance. Sometimes I joke around backstage and

Must be my agent on the line. Photo by Bert Lubin

those jokes fall flat. What I say at those times is, "Not funny backstage, funny out there." It is uncanny, but it seems to often happen to me that the flatness of my backstage humor turns into something successful when I am in front of the audience. Is that The Zone revealing itself in a different way? (By the way, being funny as hell backstage does not preclude me from having success or lack thereof in performance.)

The mysteries of comedy sure do keep things interesting.

On September 11, 2001, Dick Monday, Tiffany Riley, and I were stunned like the rest of the world by that infamous day. The Big Apple Circus went ahead with our planned dress rehearsal of "Big Top Doo Wop," just eighty miles north of New York City. It was impossibly upsetting for us to try to entertain the two hundred people who showed up to view the circus that evening. Trying to make them laugh was out of the question.

For the next three months, as we played Virginia and New York City, being a part of the Big Apple Circus clown alley galvanized us. We knew our value as clowns more clearly than ever before: to bring people together, to help them escape from emotional wreckage, and to give them permission to celebrate life again. More than ever before, we required ourselves to be in The Zone every single moment that we had a chance to entertain the Big Apple Circus audience. Our gift to Virginia and New York City that autumn and winter was The Zone.

Television is bad for you, but good for them.

The Big C and Me

In the spring of 2008, I went in for an ultrasound because I had a swollen salivary gland, and my doctor in New Jersey thought it would be a good idea. From that test, it was discovered that I had something growing on my thyroid: a small nodule. I had no symptoms, and was actually quite lucky that this test, which was both benign and unrelated to the condition of my thyroid, revealed the possibility of a bigger problem. The doctor then ordered a biopsy of my nodule to find out more about it. I was pleased that the salivary gland thing was not serious, and I was very worried that the thyroid thing was. (What the hell is a thyroid, anyway?) When I got the results of my salivary gland test, I was overseas. I told my doctor that I was going to be gone for a few weeks for some work and asked if this biopsy could wait. He said, "Enjoy Europe." I knew that the diagnosis lay ahead, but I put it far back into the recesses of my mind so I could enjoy my summer.

When I returned, I went for what was called a "fine needle aspiration." It was done at a clinic that performed ultrasounds, MRIs, and other diagnostic tests. This test involved putting a super-thin needle into my neck to extract some cells from the growth, and was done by a radiologist with the help of two young technicians. A needle in my neck – I was nervous. When I am nervous, I kid around. (When I am not nervous, I kid around.) The doctor and the two young ladies knew I was a clown in the circus, and to break the tension – my tension – I was making lots of jokes. The doctor did the first of the two needle insertions successfully, and it was uncomfortable, but not unbearable. I remember wondering if this process of piercing the nodule would actually allow the spread of cancer, but was assured it didn't spread that way.

The doctor was about to go into my neck again with the needle, but just before he did, I asked, "So, this is my prostate, right?"

    Silence.

    Dead silence.

    Not a sound came from the three who were performing my biopsy.

    This was not funny.

I finally had to say, "I am KIDDING." This assurance from me did nothing to alleviate their discomfort. They did the second aspira-

tion, pretty much in silence, and I left. I didn't really understand how that couldn't be funny to them, even if there is a worry among medical professionals about doing an incorrect procedure, test, or operation. There is nothing worse than removing the wrong mole, taking out the wrong lymph node, lopping off the wrong organ or limb. But, these fine folks knew I was a clown, and no more than five seconds before I made my joke, we had all been laughing and kidding around together. Not any longer.
Did they know something I didn't?

I was in rehearsals in August 2008 for the Big Apple Circus' 2008/2009 season when I called the doctor's office to get my test results. The doctor didn't talk to me, but the nurse did, who simply said, "The doctor will not give you the results over the phone; you need to come in." I explained I was very busy working 90 miles away, and could they please just give me the news over the phone. The nurse simply repeated that I needed to come into the office as soon as possible for the test results. My face went flush. I called my surgeon friend, Judy Weisman. When I explained how it was told to me, or rather how it had not been told to me, she said, "It must be cancer."

I felt all the blood leave my brain and I felt sick. I felt weak and horribly uncomfortable. I hadn't actually heard the worst, but I had heard the worst in a different way. Judy explained that this was medical protocol. You don't tell a patient over the phone they have cancer. I called the doctor back, at Judy's suggestion, and asked them to fax the test results to another doctor, at which point Judy looked at the results and called me back. It was papillary thyroid cancer. It was not something I was going to die from – that I would die from something else. She said this like it was great news. Judy said it is a slow growing tumor. "If you are going to have cancer, have this cancer," as it was relatively "good," she explained. I felt really sick now, having gotten this news directly, though I still planned on leaving rehearsals a few days later and going to the doctor to get the news

Me, Emily Lubin, Mark Gindick, Danielle Lubin, Photo by Ann Hageus.

again. Judy said these tumors sometimes aren't even removed until they have created a problem, which I was not having, and that pregnant women were allowed to go full term before worrying about removing this cancer.

Actress Cloris Leachman fixing my beads before a TV appearance, photo by Phil Thurston.

It all sounded like good news to me, but the knowledge that I had cancer felt like pretty fricken bad news. I had something horrible inside me and I couldn't do a whole lot about it except read about it, educate myself, and panic. (I am very good at the latter.)

There is a video interview of me that took place five minutes after I talked with Judy on www.circopedia.org. My friend, Dominique Jando, conducted it, without realizing what was going on. My lovely friend, Joel Dein, the Director of Communications at Big Apple Circus, did. Dominique had come a long way just for this video interview and I decided to go through with it, though Joel thought I should postpone. My mind was going a million miles an hour and my stomach was churning, but I felt that it would somehow be all right, and maybe even a good distraction. Go to that website and search Barry Lubin and you will see how I looked and maybe get a sense of how I felt at that moment in my life.

A few days later, I went to the office and got the news directly from my doctor. Thankfully, Judy had softened that blow considerably. When I was diagnosed, the producers from the television production company, Show of Force, who were shooting a yearlong PBS documentary on a season with the Big Apple Circus, heard rumors about my illness. They asked me if I would do an interview about what I was going through. What I was going through was hell; telling people made it worse. When I would share my condition with friends, their reaction was understandable, but caused me more pain, worry, stress, and grief. I felt the need to limit the number of people I told about the cancer, and of the subsequent operation; the number in that inner circle was small.

The producers understandably felt that to open myself up so publicly would no doubt be good for television, but I knew it would be bad for Barry. They tried to convince me that though this was my personal battle with cancer, its documentation might possibly help save countless lives by helping teach people about early prevention, etc. I just was trying to save my own life. I didn't want or need any more stress than I already had. They apparently sent their minions to try to manipulate me into an interview a few times just before my operation, but I saw right through it and I resented the hell out of it. I agreed to consider doing interviews after the operation, and my argument to them was that it might save lives or not, but either way the broadcast date was still two years away. They pushed. I didn't budge. Screw 'em.

Besides all that, I had a "hero complex" going on inside my brain. Ridiculously, I was acting like I could save everyone else – my family, my friends, my career, the Big Apple Circus – from pain and inconvenience. Everyone but myself. I was afraid of becoming emotionally and physically unable to continue my life, and my work as I had come to love it. The fear itself was paralyzing me. I wasn't in a relationship at the time, I loved my job, I loved my kids, I loved the people I was around, I was partnering with one of my best friends, Mark Gindick, and felt great, and now this. Shit hits the fan in its time, not our time. No one plans for cancer, even if we all might worry about it from time to time. Though I was told by my trusted medical genius friend, Judy Weisman, that this was the best kind of cancer, the C word still hung heavy over my entire existence.

I had a wonderful endocrinologist, ironically named Dr. Matthew Surgan, and when he explained to me what was happening inside my body and mentioned that this sort of thyroid cancer is very

With the amazing Harrison Ford, photo by Danielle Lubin.

Backstage at the Gershwin Theater with Brooke Shields, photo by Danielle Lubin.

slow growing, I asked if I could put off the surgery until it was more convenient for the Big Apple Circus. Hero complex at work.

He simply said, "If you were my father, I would tell you to have the surgery immediately."

That struck me as both sensible and alarming at the same time.

The hero complex I had is perhaps best described as: get me as far from my feelings as possible so I can save the rest of the world from having to feel them. I told my kids about my condition and minimized their worry as much as possible. I told the circus, and warned them that it might require me to be gone during a part of the season, and I still had no idea for how long. The Big Apple Circus people who meant the most to me – founder Paul Binder and soon-to-be Artistic Director, Guillaume Dufresnoy – were understanding and sympathetic to the situation, both personally and professionally, and also handled the business of replacing me, which is exactly the support I needed: they'd rescued me from my professional concerns. The show would go on. It seems absurd to me now, because in the scheme of things, a show is a show is a show. A life is a life. In show business, we often invest a great deal of ourselves, so the lines blur.

I was functioning in a near-100% state of fear. But I was still functioning. I made it my job to make sure no one knew that. I tried to make sure they had no fears or worries for me.
What the hell was I thinking?

I had an awareness of this absurd behavior as it was happening, but I also had an awareness that no particular way was the right way to deal with news of this magnitude. I forgave myself as I reacted dysfunctionally.

I developed the show through the remaining Big Apple Circus rehearsals, along with my partner, Mark, and the creative team, and I just did my job. It was the best therapy. The operation was scheduled so that I could rehearse and open the show in Virginia and hand it off the Matt Pauli, who was playing Grandma in shows at that time when I wasn't available. Matt was contacted and asked if he would be able to go into the show earlier than he had ever done before. Matt, being an amazing guy and real trouper, arranged to get out of some important gigs he had already lined up, and became available completely for the benefit of the show. Of course, this was a great relief to me. After rehearsing for four weeks in upstate New York, the show moved south to its first tour stop in Sterling, Virginia. I performed the opening weekend and handed off the show to Matt. I drove to New Jersey and a couple days later I was in St. Barnabas Hospital having my pre-op checkup. My soon to be ex, Roberta, and my daughter, Danielle, were with me.

    I was prepped and wheeled into the area outside the operating room. While I was sitting there waiting, I was never more scared in my entire life. The atmosphere was very professional, and though I felt like I was in good hands, I remember how "cold" the place felt – not in temperature, but in human terms. Sterile. Professional conditions must have required it. My heart was pounding, and I actually wondered if my blood pressure was going to be too high to operate. The anesthesiologist took over. I barely remember being wheeled into the operating room before passing out completely.

I cried when I woke up. I was very uncomfortable, because the stitches for a thyroidectomy were across my neck, forcing my head into a down position. To lift my chin to a normal position would have ripped my stitches, and that idea scared the hell out of me. My kids and my soon-to-be ex-wife were in the room with me, and I just felt this overwhelming sob overtake me. I was told that the operation had

Mikhail Baryshnikov, backstage at the Mayor's Arts and Culture Awards, Lincoln Center 2011. Photo by Joel Dein

been a success, and I was grateful for the good outcome, but I was also reflecting back on my life in a very morphine-induced state. Maybe it was the relief of all the months of worry. Maybe it was the release of emotions I had been holding back for the weeks between diagnosis and recovery. Whatever it was, I had a good cry. I wasn't feeling sorry for myself. I was feeling some panic, but also a sense of relief.

When my family comforted me, I took that comfort. I didn't try to say, "Oh don't worry about me, I am fine." Instead, I allowed it, and that was frankly unusual for me. (Hero complex and all.) The doctors and nurses were great, and I felt that I was in the best possible hands. The hospital portion of my recovery was expected to take place over one night and part of the next day, and that alone panicked me. My neck and shoulders were killing me from the downward position in which my head was stuck. I was having difficulty talking, breathing, eating, drinking. And worst of all, I was worried that my neck would close up on me and that I would die any second. I needed to calm down, but it was hard, because as the morphine minimized the pain, it also messed with my brain function. I was freaking out, trying not to let my family see this, and desperately worried that I would be released from the hospital too soon.

Before I went into the hospital, I found out that the Clown Care Program of Big Apple Circus, where trained clown "doctors" make bedside visits to pediatric wards, was opening at St. Barnabas Hospital the day of my operation. I knew the clown doctors who would be opening the program – Eileen Weiss and Andy Sapora – and I begged them to visit me while I was recovering. They did and it made a huge difference in my day, just as I knew it might, since I had been a clown doctor in the early days of Clown Care. They distracted me expertly. That was powerful stuff, considering how badly I was freaking out. I wanted my family to experience what they did, also. Andy and Eileen came in the morning, but my family had yet to arrive, so I asked them to return later. They returned twice more. My family enjoyed meeting them and they really were delightful in my hospital room. The third time they visited, I had started feeling pretty bad – with the medications for pain, and the sedatives and anesthesia wearing off – and I respectfully asked them to leave. I have been in that situation before, and so have they – where the patient truly is too uncomfortable or unhappy to enjoy clowns in the room at that moment. I told them I loved them as I kicked them out, and I will be forever grateful for their love, kindness, and generosity at St. Barnabas that day.

During the day, my surgeon, Dr. Richard Scharf, visited and told me that the operation was a success, and that he had basically given me a facelift with the placement of the stitches – a benefit for which there was no extra charge. For a couple of years after, people told me I looked great and obviously had lost lots of weight. I had not.

Ah, the many perks of having cancer!

On the first night of my at-home recovery back in my New Jersey apartment, I panicked big time. Because of the position in which my head was stuck, bent and looking down, I suddenly felt I could not breathe. I freaked out and called Judy Weisman, who talked me down. She smartly said, "You are talking to me, and that means you are breathing just fine. Take a few deep breaths. The doctor did a great job, and you will be uncomfortable for just a few days." I calmed down pretty fast, though I had nearly called an ambulance just before calling her. I was afraid of ripping out the stitches and exposing the inside of my neck, and that caused me to both freak out as well as eventually calm myself down.

I had to remain like that for one week, with a stiff neck, unable to see the sky without contorting into a very uncomfortable position. Dr. Scharf told me that I could go outside and walk around and find my own energy limits. He suggested I gradually build up my strength and endurance. I took a tiny walk the first day, but the second day I went too far. I was out of gas and far from my apartment, having walked alone looking down at my feet constantly, my head stuck in that position. After a long rest on someone's steps, and only mild panic, I was able to get back home. I became friendly with the neighbors both across the street and next door for the very first time. Maybe it was self-preservation and insurance of some sort: I could call out to them in a panic, if need be.

With Brian Stokes Mitchell, Bebe Neuwirth, and Nathan Lane, Photo by Joel Dein.

My strength returned little by little, and I gently pushed myself a bit more each day, though making sure not to push too far. My daughter Danielle took excellent care of me through those early days, but was also smart enough not to baby me too much.

The anesthesia kicked my ass more than anything, and unfortunately during the same week where my stitches had to remain in place. I felt really off. I was given strong painkillers, but they messed up my head. I only used them when the pain became too much. I preferred extra strength Tylenol without codeine, even though it didn't do much to alleviate the pain. I wanted my senses and brain to clear, which the anesthesia was still affecting. At the appointed time, and after the week of discomfort, I returned to my surgeon to have the stitches removed. Dr. Scharf was very kind, but he also got a big kick out of having a clown for a patient. On one post-op visit, he kept a room full of patients waiting outside while we chatted for about forty-five minutes. It was fun and we laughed quite a lot. I loved being treated like a VIP – a very important patient – but when I left his office and saw the throng of patients lined up to see Dr. Scharf, I felt terrible. Now you know why your doctors are so often behind schedule and keeping you waiting: clowns.

After that week, I went to see Dr. Chen at Overlook Hospital, who was my new doctor in charge of follow-up treatment. He explained that he was going to make me radioactive in a few weeks. WHAT? It was not what you might think of as typical radiation treatment for cancer. It was something quite interesting, I learned. Iodine goes right to thyroid tissue. If one takes a radioactive iodine pill, the iodine finds any remaining thyroid cells anywhere in the body and kills them. It is particularly

Me and Danielle Lubin with Brooke Shields, backstage at the Gershwin Theater, 2011. Photo by Joel Dein

lethal to just those cells, and has been the protocol for my kind of cancer for over four decades. After that, I would get a body scan, which would indicate how well the pill worked to eradicate any remaining cancerous cells in my body.

I went back to work two weeks after my surgery, lacking in energy, but still raring to go back into the Big Apple Circus. By then, everyone at the circus was aware of my illness and my reason for leaving suddenly. I was overwhelmed by love on my return and that felt so good. I was also overwhelmed by the knowledge that I was going to be in the ring again, which I loved so much – something for which I ached during the time of my recovery. A friend once said to me, "There are only a limited number of shows in any performer's lifetime." My number was decreased by two weeks, and I was chomping at the bit. After two days of rehearsing in the Big Top at Lincoln Center, I was back in the game. I nearly cried the first moment I stepped back into the ring. I was back and pretty darn grateful to everyone who made that possible.

A few weeks later, Matt returned to the circus to fill in for me, because it was time for me to go radioactive again. I was forced to miss a week of shows. The Show of Force television crew had asked if they could interview others at Big Apple Circus about me while I was gone the first time, and I had said it was fine. And now that I was back on the job, they were finally able to interview me. They asked if they could accompany me to my doctors and videotape the treatments and body scans, etc. I consented, because I knew it would distract me from my fears, which quickly started to rise to the surface again. In one day, I had to go to the hospital three separate times. The last time was to receive the radioactive pill, and once I took that, I couldn't be near anyone for several days without potentially giving him or her a big dose of radioactivity. I found it fascinating that even the wall in the apartment I shared with Danielle wasn't enough, so she moved out for a few days. And for months, when traveling, I had to take a note with me because I could potentially set off sensors in airports.

What would I do if the scans indicated that the operation and the radioactive iodine pill hadn't been 100% successful at eradicating my cancer?

How would I be able to deal with my claustrophobia while in the machine getting scanned?

Am I going die?

All these questions flowed in and out of my brain, mixed in with tons of denial. I tried to educate myself as much as possible about the disease, the treatment, percentages, and the long-term prognosis. I got to the point where I realized I didn't understand it very well at all, so I placed myself in the hands of the professionals who did.

The television crew followed me around that day when I was at the hospital three times, and the doctors and technicians were very generous, and allowed them into places rarely visited by camera crews. It distracted me from my worries – mission accomplished – and they got lots of footage, some of which was eventually used in the PBS series, Circus. At the end of the third visit, I was given this radioactive iodine pill and was left alone because of safety issues. I left the hospital feeling odd, because there was no sensation of radioactivity, no nausea, no obvious change whatsoever. I just felt normal. I drove myself home to my apartment, and for the next three days I was alone. Danielle, Emily, and Roberta left meals on the porch each day, and I would wave at them from a distance while I became less and less radioactive.

I was pretty upset, however, that I didn't glow in the dark

A few days later, I went in for a body-scan. I became very claustrophobic and panicky, and at one point asked the technician to stop the diagnostic test. Then, I was able to pull myself together and finish. I was unable to go anywhere near the show for one week, since I was still giving off radiation, and because the circus audience is made up of many children and some pregnant women. When that week was up, and after Matthew did a great job of replacing me and partnering with Mark again, I returned to the ring.

With Bello Nock and Richard Gere, and Kevin Venardos behind Bello's hair. Photo by Jennifer Nock

I got this form of cancer, known as papillary thyroid cancer, at an advanced age compared to most, and because of my age I will never be considered cured. Isn't it interesting that someone twenty years younger than me, having gone through exactly the same diagnosis, operation, radioactive treatment, and diagnostic tests, would now be considered cured? But not me.

I have been told that I must remain vigilant for life, and that means regular blood tests, ultrasounds, and examinations. I don't like having to live with this for the rest of my life, but I am so grateful that it was caught very early, and totally by chance, giving me the best possible chance for survival.

One of my best friends from Big Apple Circus was the musical director and trumpet player Rob Slowik. He knew the gravity of the situation, but he managed to crack me up repeatedly. When I was complaining about something work related, which I often did anyway, Rob would ask, "Are you playing the cancer card?" I would dissolve into fits of laughter, though I knew someone who didn't understand the friendship that I had with Rob would probably be offended if they had overheard. I was so happy for the laughs and Rob's ironic sense of humor when I needed it most.

In times like these, when your life is on the line, you know who your true friends are. I am blessed to say I have a lot of friends.

Instructions are like words which tell you how to put stuff together.

Seeing the World on Someone Else's Dime

Long ago, back in 1974 when I auditioned for Clown College at the old Boston Garden, I had the opportunity to talk to a working clown, a lovely man and great clown by the name of Jim Howle. He generously gave me, and the young woman with whom I'd been paired, lots of fascinating information. One of the coolest things he talked about was traveling around America and seeing the country from a different perspective than from highways and byways. Jim explained that if I were lucky enough to get a job with the circus, not only would I experience the U.S. by seeing America's backyards, but I would do so on Ringling's dime. How cool is that!

That idea appealed to me, because I grew up wanting to travel. It was one of my dreams to see the world. How lucky was I that my first professional job started fulfilling that dream? On the Ringling Circus train, we traveled constantly and I saw lots of cities, mountains, oceans, valleys, forests, and backyards of America. There was a town in Ohio where, each year, the entire population would come out to watch the circus train travel by. We passed through their town at forty miles an hour, but the thrill was evident as they waved wildly at us, hoping for a view of a clown, a horse, an elephant, for just the briefest of moments. During my five tours with Ringling, I saw nearly every big city, state, and national park in the nation while traveling on the circus train. On their dime.

Doing the Step and Repeat thing at the Gershwin Theater with Danielle Lubin. Photo by Robert Soifer

I loved train travel so much that during the off-season, while the rest of the cast and crew would head home or go on vacation, I would purchase an Amtrak rail pass and travel on all the routes across America, getting on and off on a whim. For instance, I got off the train in Reno, Nevada, played blackjack for twelve hours, and caught the next train to San Francisco. I loved it that much. A couple of times in recent years, I talked with the producers of Ringling about going back to work there as a headliner, after years of performing on other shows. When the subject of the train was broached, they wouldn't commit to a comfortable space for my family and me for the fifty-week tour. That was a deal breaker.

I managed to see forty-eight states on Ringling's dime, Alaska on Holland America Cruise Line's dime, and only Hawaii on my own dime. I have set foot on six continents, nearly all on someone else's dime. I work, live in, and travel throughout Europe regularly. I have been to Saipan in the South Pacific, Japan, Taiwan, Russia, Brazil, Argentina, Uruguay, Ghana, the Canary Islands, South Africa, New Zealand, and Kazakhstan. Someone else paid for it, and in fact paid me to travel to those countries as well. I still want to go to new and interesting places in the world on someone's generous dime. It will most likely be on my own dime when I visit Antarctica, unless someone can offer me a gig there.

Just for fun, I once made a list of all the countries I have been to. As of this writing, I have visited thirty-eight. Where else would I like to go? China, Israel, Tanzania, Kenya, India, Nepal, Indonesia, Chile, Columbia, Singapore, Panama, Antarctica, Thailand, Egypt, Australia, Vietnam, Cambodia, Malaysia, and more, please.

Brother, can you spare a dime?

Live each day to the fullest, then find a way to relieve the bloating.

Failures

Failure is a big part of clowning, and probably most businesses and art forms. They say: with great risk comes great reward. They neglect to mention that it also comes with a lot of pain, humiliation, self-doubt, loss of sleep, and much, much more! (Who are they, anyway?) I have managed to fail on the biggest stage in the circus business, and yet I am in the Ring of Fame in Sarasota, the highest honor in the American Circus. I failed on a recent paid gig in which I clowned aboard a ship, but then again, I am an inductee in the International Clown Hall of Fame. So, what is failure, exactly, and what does it mean to me? Failure wakes us up in the best possible way. It's a great motivator, I believe. We have to handle failure well in order to succeed.

There is no other way to try out new material than to take the risk in front of a live audience. I am amazed at how often I am wrong about an idea which I was sure would be a good one. The audience informed me otherwise. I am amazed at how that still amazes me after all these years. I should know better by now, yet every time I think a gag is great and it fails, it blows my mind.

For instance…the Superman Gag.

The gag was great, we thought. It starred the funniest clown on Ringling Brothers and Barnum & Bailey, Peter Pitofsky, to whom an entire chapter could be devoted. Peter was a gangly, super-rubber-faced, no-holds-barred physical genius. He was also a clown's clown, meaning someone we could all count on in clown alley to make us laugh. Not an easy chore. Peter was cast as Superman. I was Grandma being robbed by a clown dressed as a crook. Peter, dressed as Clark Kent, sees the crime being perpetrated, tries to find a place to change, sees a phone booth, and discovers the door is jammed. Then Peter runs around it as fast as he can, as if that will prevent him from being seen. Meanwhile, I am being robbed and robbed and robbed some more, as Peter tries to change clothes not inside the phone booth, but as he is running around it. This causes massive clothing failure, lots of tripping, pants around ankles, shirt covering his face as he tries taking it off, and finally he turns into Superman. It takes Peter so long to change into Superman that the robber has finished the job of taking everything I own and exits.

The end.

It made the entire two-hundred-person cast of Ringling laugh the night before our first paid audience that season. I was so proud to be a part of it. Yet, it wasn't deemed funny enough; it got cut, and no audience ever saw it. Devastating.

Oklahoma.

The Oklahoma sketch, which I developed, and in which I directed clowns Jeff Gordon and Tom Dougherty for a Big Apple Circus show, was a similar failure. That routine was based on the absurdity (to me) of Dinner Theater. This is a very American thing, where mostly middle-aged and elderly people are served a meal, then watch a semi-professional version of a famous Broadway musical or play from their tables. For a satire of this "art form," I created a very simple concept for these two very talented clowns, who were working together for a Big Apple Circus season. The idea was that one of them simply said to the audience, "And now,

They made a cookie out of me, with Ann Hageus, photo by Danielle Lubin.

dinner theater," and proceeded to belt out the theme song to the famous Broadway musical, "Oklahoma." The comedy idea was that as they sang out the song with great enthusiasm, they ate a plateful of peas and mashed potatoes. As you can imagine, there was an explosion of food at key moments. This routine was carefully rehearsed so that no one would see it in its early stages, and it was rolled out to the powers that be, director, producer, and cast of Big Apple Circus a week before opening. To me it was side-splittingly funny and a source of great pride. It was a good example of keeping it simple: two guys eating peas and mashed potatoes, singing an American classic. It was cut. It was deemed too juvenile. No audience has ever seen this routine. (Yet...)

Working The Palace.

Another significant failure, which I eventually turned into a success, was performing at the Palace at Auburn Hills. The first time I played a giant three-ring arena circus solo, post-Ringling, was at one of the most beautiful basketball and concert meccas in America, in the Detroit suburb of Auburn Hills, aptly named The Palace. Royal Hanneford Circus was playing there, and though it was a venue with 22,000 seats, it was full nearly every show. The engagement for which I was hired ran from Thursday through Sunday, with two shows each day, and three on Saturday. I had done several successful stints with Royal Hanneford over the previous few years, but always in their one-ring Big Top tent with a capacity of 1,600 seats. This was a big step up for me, but if the producers, Tommy and Struppi Hanneford, felt that I could handle it, then perhaps I was ready.

I had been inspired by the success that the great Italian clown, David Larible, had with Ringling. He starred on the big three-ring arena show for several seasons, working solo at times, and with audience volunteers. He learned how to play big without losing his character or his comedy timing, and his background was nearly 100% European one-ring circus. I had done a little solo work while on Ringling, where I had the attention of the entire arena and all the spotlights for a few moments, with some success. By that, I mean that I made the entire audience of fifteen- to twenty-thousand laugh, but in very short bursts. I saw that it could be done throughout an entire performance; inspired by David Larible, I wanted to try it. I took the booking.

I was a nervous wreck, and that was before realizing how many people would attend each show. The ticket prices were so reasonable that anyone in this heavily populated suburb of Detroit could attend the circus for around the same price as a movie ticket. I arrived the day before the engagement to rehearse, and I was ready for the matinee, with 22,000 people in attendance, on Thursday morning.

I died. I got nothing from the audience. No response.

I went back to the drawing board and changed a few things around.

Thursday night, 22,000 people: nothing. Flop sweat, fear, the

With Danielle Lubin and Princess Stephanie of Monaco at the Circus Festival in 2008. Photo by Marc Koltnow, Sr.

pain of knowing I was letting down the producers, and the pain of not getting any laughs.
For Friday, I'd have to go back to the drawing board.
Friday morning: nothing.
Friday afternoon, back to the drawing board for even more changes.
Friday night: NOTHING!
Saturday morning, the first of three shows: nothing.
Back to the drawing board, more changes.
Saturday, second show...
I hit. That comedy term simply means I succeeded. In fact, the sound of the audience reactions to me was overwhelming. I literally stopped performing as I felt the response wash over me from both sides of the huge arena. I have tried to describe the feeling, but it's impossible to fully convey. The sound of laughter coming from every direction just washed over me. The hair on the back of my neck stood up. And then, an emotion I had never before felt in performance hit me – pure euphoria – and I suddenly understood, or at least imagined, how a rock star must feel. Thankfully, I returned to sanity after a long pause and continued my performance. Center ring, twelve spotlights following my every move, an audience response sending chills up and down my spine, the ultimate acceptance.

Saturday night's show was the same.

Sunday, both shows, the same.

I had seemingly figured it out. When under great stress and pressure, mysterious things sometime happen, and through trial and error I have made it work. Maybe not the first show, but eventually. Sooner rather than later is my preference, but it isn't always in the cards. I will never forget that first moment of working solo at The Palace, finally making 22,000 people laugh in unison.

Wrestling.

The Wrestling Gag failure occurred during my early years at the Big Apple Circus when we had what was called "The Group." We never personally called it that, but we found out a decade later that, in Europe, we were being followed by various clowns and circus fans who found our trio to be "important" in their world and our world. The trio consisted of Michael Christensen, who was Mr. Stubbs; Jeff Gordon, known as "Mr. Gordoon"; and myself. Together, we did some pretty nice work. We would "noodle" ideas, a term Michael created for the process of putting something together for the first time. (Michael was famous for starting the hospital program that brought clowns for bedside visits in pediatric wards, and which has grown worldwide, called Clown Care.) Michael was just beginning to explore and discover the perfect

With Erdeo Pellegrini at the International Circus Festival of Kazakhstan 2013, Photo by Cara Muturganov.

character for himself: a tramp clown – a character who had a few tricks up his sleeve, who was smarter than you might guess, and who simply loved to share his joy of life. Jeff kept a notebook of his ideas, which might remind someone of Da Vinci's books of scientific drawings. He was and is a very creative person who might have seven hundred thoughts that lead to one fantastic idea.

Jeff is famous for creating the toilet paper routine, where he placed a hand-held role of TP at the end of a leaf blower and sent it flying through the air in beautiful, ever-changing patterns. Sadly, it has been stolen by dozens upon dozens of clowns worldwide. My wife and I were there and observed Jeff creating this magic, which no one had ever done before. They say imitation is the highest form of flattery. I say, stealing is the highest form of flatulence.

During rehearsals one season, we asked the largest man in the circus, the bottom man in a Polish teeterboard troupe, if he would participate in a gag where he wrestled Grandma. The guy was easily 6-foot-5, and weighed a minimum of three hundred pounds. We rehearsed it and laughed our asses off each time.

Then we did it for a live audience and got no response.

We tried it over and over, changing things along the way to try to save it, improve it, make work what we were so sure would work.

Nothing. Dismal failure.

We quickly went to work on a new piece to replace this

disaster and it was a fabulous success. Failure and pain led us toward something magical. What had to exist from the start was a desire to make a successful routine, which pleased the audience and was a lot of fun for the trio to perform. Though we haven't worked as a trio in over two decades, we can all still make each other laugh just by mentioning the wrestling gag. Michael and I also have referred to it as "Jeff's Gag," which is our way of kidding around with the man who is actually the most inventive of the three, but who has come up with some pretty bad ideas before settling on that one great idea you remember forever.

The Miss Lincoln Center Pageant routine was a dismal failure. Working with Big Apple Circus was difficult in many ways, yet very satisfying when successful, which is not often an easy task. The great difficulty of working a circus in repertory, which is playing to nearly the same audience year in and year out, requires constant change. Most clowns in the circus world perfect a few acts and then change venues constantly, allowing them to repeat material every season. There are some very successful clowns who do just that, and they return to places they have played after a few years again and again. I performed for twenty-five seasons with Big Apple Circus, and had to do something different every year. And though there were not 100% returnees at each show, it was a very high percentage, simply because the Big Apple Circus has an extremely loyal audience, and for good reason: it is a great circus year in and year out and it changes every single season…unlike Cirque du Soleil, with all due respect, which tours a show for well over a decade, or remains stationary in Las Vegas or Orlando, with the same show for many years.

For the winter season of 1986, I created a routine called "The Miss Lincoln Center Pageant," a parody of various beauty pageants like Miss America, Miss World, Miss Universe, etc. I find pageants to be both silly and fun. I grew up in Atlantic City with the annual Miss America Pageant broadcast from my hometown every year. Even at a young age, I found it thrilling that Miss America was crowned right in my own backyard. My family and I would try to guess the winner every year; we were rarely correct. We always went up to the boardwalk for the Miss America Parade as the contestants passed by in convertibles before going on to compete for the coveted crown the remainder of the week. I'm not afraid to say that I always cried when the winner was crowned, and the incomparable Bert Parks sang the iconic song, "There She is, Miss America."

I fashioned in my head what I believed would be a great idea based off my childhood memories of pageants. I (well, Grandma) would run for Miss Lincoln Center! (Lincoln Center being the cultural capital of New York made this idea more absurd.) The gag was I was going to run for Miss Lincoln Center unopposed… and lose. My talent was going to be basketball. I rigged a small hoop and basketball so that I could dunk in slow motion; with a string on my finger, I could slow the ball as much as I wanted. Strobe lights would help to accentuate the scene. I wore something very drab, almost matching my usual red dress for the evening gown competition, and for the swimsuit competition – and this is still embarrassing to think about decades later – I wore a leopard bikini over my dress. I paraded around like a fashion model. At the end, Ringmaster Paul Binder, the "Bert Parks" of this seemingly endless debacle, opened the envelope as the drummer played the requisite drum roll.

And I "lost."

The entire sketch was so bad I wanted to take it out back behind the tent and shoot it.

It didn't work for several reasons. For one, I was trying to fulfill what I believed the press would appreciate and review well, which is folly. I work for the audience, not a newspaper reviewer. The most important thing: it probably didn't resonate with the family audience. The reference was near and dear to me, but not to them. Finally, it simply wasn't funny. That is the cardinal rule of comedy. It is the very definition of comedy. If it isn't funny, that is a failure by all standards. It was basically crap; a missed short field goal; a third-strike bunt attempt; crap. Did I mention it was crap?

If you are going to fail, make it a doozy. I have had a lot of doozies, but got up and succeeded. And I'm sure I'll have a lot more along the way.

> **Politics is the intersection of serious thought and that street with the funny name in Altoona.**

Regrets

I have heard it said that we should leave this world without any regrets, and I have heard people say that if you have no regrets, you haven't lived. Talk about contradictions. At least I have succeeded according to one of those criteria, because I have regrets.

I regret not being there more for my daughters as they were growing up. There was a period of time when I was running from my responsibilities – a time when I was using lots of ways to escape from my feelings. Work, drugs, gambling, eating, and other things that removed me from the world's difficulties for a fleeting moment. This behavior also removed me somewhat from their lives. And now I make sure to tell them every time we talk that I love them, and every time I see them, I hug them.

I regret turning down a career as a music video director, an offer made to me by Paris Barclay, who has gone on to dizzying heights as a director in Hollywood. Paris hired me to create and direct the comedy segments of a music video he was directing for a now-defunct rock group. I had a blast doing the two-day gig. The musicians were totally game for the fun and comedy, and I felt like it was a success. It was during these two days that Paris made me the offer. I was stunned, and I stammered a bit, but answered, "I would love to do that…after following you around for a year." He replied brusquely, "No, you are ready for it now. Your work is entirely visual; this work is entirely visual. Do you want the job or not?" I turned it down. I was both flattered and flabbergasted that he offered me this job working for his New York production company, Black and White TV. My biggest reason for turning it down was less about inexperience, more about the pure intimidation. I felt awkward being around big-time music company executives and the management team of the band. During the two-day shoot, Paris navigated those shark-infested waters beautifully because he had the right temperament and knew how and when to say no. I was pretty sure I would be eaten alive. Would I have done things differently, if given the chance? Frankly, yes.

I regret turning down a chance to perform as the only clown on an all-star circus that was going to tour the entire world – The Monte Carlo Circus – which was comprised of winners of the International Circus Festival of Monte Carlo, and me. It was the opportunity of a lifetime to see so much more of the world, and to work alongside the greats of the circus world. But, at that time, I wasn't ready, and I knew it, even though the producers saw it differently. Opportunity knocked, no one answered.

I promised myself years ago that I would regret as little as possible for the rest of my days. I resolved to do this when I was reminded on 9/11 that life is short. Opportunities come in many forms

With Kathryn O'Dell, the woman instrumental into my induction into the International Clown Hall of Fame in 2002. Photo by Aye Jaye

and present themselves not in my time, but in their own. I consider myself a very conservative person, which surprises people who look at what I do for a living and where I have traveled. A part of me wants to hide from the world – to sit at home and take the safest path. Though I travel constantly, I am a lousy traveler and an even worse eater; yet, I tend to take work in high-pressure situations, in strange and unpredictable parts of the world, with people I have never met before.

Welcome to show business.

From the moment I sign a new deal, I immediately try to figure out a way to get out of it, worrying the entire time, leading up to my departure, about the gig, the food, the flights, the money exchange, and EVERYTHING. Inevitably, I find a way to succeed, and to be quite happy that I didn't "chicken out" and miss a great life experience.

Several years ago, I decided I was sick and tired of traveling and didn't want to be uncomfortable ever again. After two weeks, I realized that to do so would mean missing out on the world and all it had to offer. I am so glad I didn't succumb to my comfort zone. Instead, I listen to my heart.

No regrets…just occasional bad food.

Fame

I want to talk about fame.

I consider myself a low-level famous person, and even then, only in certain American markets. The two biggest cities – New York and Boston – happen to be amazing places for me. Over the years, I have had friends introduce me as a famous clown when I was out of costume and makeup. Most of the time, the reaction is strange looks followed by "um," "uh," "ok…" or something like that. I have learned to say, at those moments, "If you have to introduce me as being famous, I'm not famous."

A mutual friend of phenomenal magic icons Penn and Teller was walking around with me in the suburbs of Milwaukee and continuously introducing me as Teller…while the real Teller stood next to me the entire time.

I do love irony.

Penn once wrote, "I don't like clowns, but if I had to like one, it would be Grandma." That, to me, was a great honor coming from him.

When I was young, I often dreamed of being on television, in the movies, on radio, getting reviewed in The New York Times, being written about in that newspaper's Sunday Arts & Leisure section. Now I can say I have been in a few movies, made lots of national television appearances, was featured in a series about the circus that was broadcast on every continent, have been featured in many other international broadcasts, and done tons of local television, press, interviews, and radio appearances. I have been featured in The New York Times a few times and have been part of full-page ads in that and many other newspapers and magazines. I have been in People and Us Magazines, reviewed makeup in Glamour, and had a feature about me in Maxim. (Yes, Maxim.) Thrilling to me for sure, but I'm still not really famous. Some might disagree, and bless them for that, but I will still call myself a low-grade famous person/celebrity. And even at that, Grandma is the celebrity, not me.

Fame is Harrison Ford. He came to the Big Apple Circus and our publicists placed me in a position to be photographed with him, to which he graciously agreed. The flashes from the dozen or so paparazzi were so numerous that it was like one giant unending lightening flash, and I was certain at that moment that this sort of thing must happen all the time to Mr. Ford. He smiled and gave the photographers what they wanted, and then he got to a point where he felt that they had taken enough photos and said, "Okay, folks." The photographers just kept flashing and he had to say in a much stronger tone, "OKAY!" He had given them what they needed, but they weren't ready to stop. Honestly, fame like that scares me.

My publicists from Big Apple Circus, and Ringling Brothers and Barnum & Bailey, paved the way to helping me achieve this low-level fame, and I have worked with great ones. Quite a few have told me that I am my own best P.R. man. Joel Dein, the Director of Communications at Big Apple Circus, always theorized that if people were paying lots of attention to Grandma, they were much more likely to buy tickets to the Big Apple Circus. Joel got me a TON of attention in many major markets in the eastern U.S., got me booked on numerous national television shows, and along with Phil Thurston, the P.R. manager of the circus, I was put forward on anything big or small that came along which might help sell tickets and reach new potential customers. Their great efforts really helped get Grandma's name and face out there. Whenever I am with Joel and someone recognizes me, I always point at Joel and say, "It's his fault."

Fame is Michael Jackson coming to the Big Apple Circus with "junk bond king" Michael Milken, a man who had spent time in prison for Wall Street improprieties. They were together in New York for a charity event and came to the circus with a few hundred kids from that charity. The audience was barely watching the circus. They had their eyes on Michael Jackson. Frankly, so did the entire cast and crew. The most surreal moment for me was when I was doing a bit which involved Grandma dancing and I realized I was dancing for the pleasure (hopefully) of one of the all-time greatest dancers and entertainers in show business history.

Fame is Tom Cruise, David Beckham, Katie Holmes, and Victoria "Posh Spice" Beckham sitting in the front row at Big Apple Circus. No paparazzi were allowed inside the Big Top, and no one gave the press any notice that they were there. The circus had to make accommodations for them to have separate bathrooms from the public, for fear the audience would inundate them with autograph and photo requests. So, they were walked through the ring to their front row seats before the show, and during intermission, they were walked from their seats to the back of the tent to use the facilities, and then back to their seats just prior to the start of the second half. This drew incredible amounts of attention to them, but otherwise they were simply able to enjoy the circus. Of course, all eyes from the audience, and the cast and crew, were on them. I could have made a mint just taking a photo of them inside the Big Top and selling it to various press outlets. But I didn't.

Years before, just after the release of his film, Born on the Fourth of July, I met Mr. Cruise backstage at a show I was in, and I asked him, "Can I borrow your career?" He laughed. I am not sure I would like to trade places with Tom, other than being a world-famous action film star, multi-millionaire, and film producer. He can have the rest.

I never did achieve mass recognition through acting in film or on television; I convinced myself that it was better this way – that I probably couldn't have handled it, anyway. On the other hand, I have undeniably achieved some level of fame. Step into the ring of the Big Apple Circus at the start of a performance and I instantly get cheers, and not just the polite kind. I have had entire audiences chanting, "Grandma! Grandma! Grandma!" – totally unsolicited, and it always thrilled and kind of embarrassed me. Though, as any circus producer will tell you, the circus is the star, not any one individual.

I have walked down the streets of New York City and Boston dressed in character, and was recognized quite often. People would instantly shout out, "Grandma!" It meant they knew the character, and that always made me smile. I have been in well over a dozen Macy's Thanksgiving Day Parades over the years, where I received many warm responses from the crowd while the parade was passing down Central Park West on the Upper West Side of Manhattan. It was often so overwhelming at times that my cheeks started to hurt from smiling and tears would stream down my face.

On the other side of fame, I appeared inside the Big Apple Circus ring one time, full house, and got absolutely no response. The occasion was the debut in our ring of Britney Spears' "Circus," sung by the superstar herself. The ABC show, Good Morning America (GMA) chose to broadcast their entire two-hour national morning program from our tent, with the second hour devoted to

Britney's appearance. I was hired by GMA to appear in the first hour to do something fun to entertain the millions at home eagerly anticipating Britney's performance, and to also liven up the audience inside the Big Top. To be honest, they didn't need any livening up. The tickets for the event were offered by lottery. The place was packed at 6 a.m. for the 7 a.m. start of GMA, and the Big Top was abuzz, to say the least. I was introduced by the hosts of the show, walked into the ring, and got zero response – not the slightest hint of recognition. I was trumped by the enormous fame of Britney Spears. My bit, which I worked out in advance with the hosts of GMA, was to claim that I was actually Britney Spears, and to boast that the audience was there, in fact, to see me.

It certainly didn't matter.

I was just one of several opening acts for Ms. Spears that morning; thankfully, none of the others seem to go over that well, either. She finally appeared, and of course, it was bedlam.

Fame is also Mikhail Baryshnikov standing alone backstage at a charity event and being completely accessible to anyone who wanted to talk or say hello. For some reason he knew who I was, which floored me. At this same event, Alec Baldwin held a Grandma doll in his arms as Mayor Michael Bloomberg of New York City lovingly talked about me to the full house at Alice Tully Hall at Lincoln Center. That sort of thing caused some people to feel that I was famous at that moment. I almost believed it myself.

Bedlam was when Derek Jeter, New York Yankees superstar, appeared in the Big Apple Circus ring with a sold-out audience there for his charity, Turn Two Foundation. I volunteered to do a comic bit with Derek and met him before the show. In that show, I was doing a trick with a giant hula-hoop. I suggested Mr. Jeter do that in front of his very favorable crowd and I explained it was quite easy to do. He is a pretty shy person and he declined, feeling that this was my trick and not his. Frankly, this trick is easier than just using a regular size hula-hoop. Once the performance ended, the audience stayed, because they were told something very special was about to happen. Derek walked out in front of the crowd and they went completely crazy. Insanity is the best word to describe what happened next. With the adrenaline rush he got from just showing up, he reached behind to where I was standing, grabbed the giant hula-hoop from me, and swung it around his waist and nailed the trick. Zero practice. The audience frenzy went up ten notches. The hair on the back of my neck stood up, and joyful chaos reigned inside the Big Top. Fame like that can make you temporarily deaf.

Fame was Chris Chambliss, a huge sports hero with the New York Yankees of the '70s and a batting coach of the team, looking sad at an autograph-signing event with the newly crowned 1996 World Series-winning Yankees. The autograph lines for the players were long and feverishly excited. Mr. Chambliss' line was almost non-existent. Fame can be short lived.

On the field at Boston's Fenway Park Opening Day 2005 with Dinny McGuire, photo by Joel Dein.

I sat between Baseball Hall of Famers Don Drysdale and Tommy John at a two-hour charity autograph session the New York Daily News had sponsored. I had a grand total of seven people interested in my signature, while the lines were enormous for the two sports legends. The fun for me was making small talk with these two gentlemen, since I had little else to do. Every once in a while, one of them would suggest to a fan to get my autograph, too, which the fans did…reluctantly.

There is no Grandma baseball card…yet.

The first celebrities I met were Betty White and Allen Ludden, although working on Atlantic City's Steel Pier afforded me the chance to serve a few slices of pizza or snow cones to some famous folk. I was a First-of-May (first-year) clown with Ringling Brothers and Barnum & Bailey Circus, and my job was to escort two of the many stars in attendance during opening night at a Los Angeles benefit performance for Project Hope, a floating hospital that sailed around the world to serve people in need. Allen and Betty couldn't have been nicer to me and I was thrilled. Betty kept asking me what it was like to travel and work in the circus, and I was happy to chat with them. I escorted them down the giant ramp leading from outside the Fabulous Forum and into the center ring, until they were introduced to great applause by the nineteen thousand in attendance. As we walked down the ramp, people were lining the sides taking photographs, both paparazzi and regular folk. Flashbulbs went off aplenty for each of the celebs. Once we arrived at center ring, I was asked to go back outside to the top of the ramp in case any other late arriving celebs needed escorting. There were none, but just for fun – when it was time for me to return to the arena – I walked back down the ramp solo and waved at the photographers' line it like I were a movie star. Confused, some of them actually took pictures, and at that moment I felt like a star. I was laughing to myself, though, when I thought about their inevitable confusion as they developed the photos later on and asked, "Who the hell is that?"

At a charity event a couple of years ago, I invited my daughter Danielle to join me. I thought she would be thrilled at the chance to meet some of her favorite stars, most of all Daniel Radcliffe. Before the event, there was a dinner across the street that we were invited to attend, and on our way back inside the theater, the organizer of the event asked if Danielle and I would like to pose on the red carpet for the press. I wasn't in costume, but did dress well for the pre-show party. We did what is known as "Step and Repeat." You pose in front of one set of photographers, then move a few feet and pose for another set, and so on. The photographers were most kind to Danielle and me, and we all knew that none of these photos would be placed in any publication or website any place on earth. Danielle and I had a ball, and when we completed the process, we entered the theater and I changed into Grandma to get ready for the charity performance.

With Steve Smith, many times my director, and Bernice Collins, clown, and wonderful person who many times I shared a dressing room with on Ringling. Photo by Lyle Fodge

During the performance, we chatted backstage with the

hosts, one of whom was Brooke Shields, who couldn't have been nicer to Danielle and me. Finally, it was time for my appearance, which included giving an award to the former star of Law and Order: SVU's Chris Meloni for his children's charity work. Unexpectedly, when I handed him his award, Chris dipped and kissed me. Fame sometimes means just being near fame, and I was near enough to know that Chris Meloni's beard was scratchy.

Fame is having my name and Grandma's name mentioned annually on NBC's national television broadcast to sixty-five million viewers of the Macy's Thanksgiving Day Parade. My kids would watch every year for the thrill of seeing me, and hearing the hosts talk about me on NBC. Sometimes it was just five seconds of exposure, sometimes thirty seconds – though one time I did get three minutes! There is also the thrill of appearing in front of three to six million spectators lining the parade route. I always hoped that NBC caught me on camera, and hoped to hear my name mentioned, but one year they didn't. I changed positions for the entertainment of the live crowds down the parade route and stupidly didn't get back into the right placement for the NBC cameras where they expected me to be. Oops!

I always called Parade Day my favorite day of the year. After my career with Big Apple Circus ended, the following Thanksgiving I was sailing on a ship on the Amazon River in Brazil dining with the U.S. Ambassador. I couldn't have been much further from New York City at that moment, but a tear came to my eye as I thought about what I was missing that day on the freezing cold streets of New York City and on televisions all over America, including my children's. In my last season on Big Apple Circus, I was invited to be a guest at a special event that Macy's chose to hold in the ring of the Big Apple Circus on one of our off-nights. They served lovely food and gave awards to some of their employees for their cherished service over many years. And then, I was honored with an award, which totally caught me by surprise. I received the Legend of the Parade Award, only the fifth time it was given in the eighty-seven-year history of the Macy's Thanksgiving Day Parade. Yes, I cried – sobbed, in fact.

In greasepaint, I was certainly recognized as Grandma during the performances of the Big Apple Circus. Heck, I was on all the banners, posters, ads, and programs – hard not to recognize me. At the end of the show, I could quickly remove my makeup and join the audience as they exited without being noticed. Occasionally people would acknowledge me, but rarely. I often rode the subway after a show with many audience members, easily identifiable by their Big Apple Circus souvenirs. I always hoped to overhear someone talking about Grandma, and once in a while, I did. Delightful!

Irony is what happened to me when an act from Big Apple Circus was booked to be on a famous national television show, Live with Regis and Kelly. I got a ticket so I could watch my friends on the show from the studio audience. (Not in character, of course.) Just before the circus act was to perform, Regis and Kelly had a contest where they called someone from the audience at home and asked them a question – which the hosts made so simple, and with so many hints, that the person at home couldn't possibly get it wrong – and that person won a prize. Once they gave the correct answer, the person at home was asked to pick a number from one to one hundred, because there were one hundred numbered seats in the studio audience. The person's seat that was picked would also win that day's prize, which was a microwave oven. That number happened to correspond with my seat number; the cameras zoomed in on me and I jumped up excitedly, happy to win and to be on television. The very next image on millions of television screens was the program of that year's Big Apple Circus with me as Grandma on the cover, as the announcer said, "Coming up next on Live with Regis and Kelly: from the Big Apple Circus, the Rios Brothers." No one knew but me that I had just been on live TV as myself, followed instantly by a photo of Grandma filling the screen. It was a surreal moment… and I got fifty bucks for selling the microwave the next day.

I walked away from the one place on this earth where, as the Cheers theme song goes, "You want to go where everybody knows your name." The Big Apple Circus was that place. Chevy Chase was quoted as saying that he became more famous than the other "not-ready-for-primetime players" during his one season on Saturday Night Live because his name was mentioned every episode. "I'm Chevy Chase and you're not." In nearly every show, the Ringmaster would call me Grandma, and I believe that helped make me better-known to the audience, and the fact that I appeared for twenty-five seasons certainly helped, too.

Julia Roberts, who ironically played a big movie star in the film Notting Hill, said to Hugh Grant, the simple owner of a bookstore, "You know, the fame thing is not real." From the outside looking in, it looks real to me, and from my perspective it is fleeting. I live quite anonymously in Sweden. It probably helps that I don't wear the makeup and dress when I leave the house, but if I did in Stockholm, nothing, nada, nil, zilch recognition. I walked out of a circus show in Sweden a few weeks ago and no one knew who I was. It was an odd feeling, and one that would have been unusual in the U.S.

Romeo the Epic Cat. Photo by Emily Lubin

I have been lucky enough to have the opportunity to talk to some of the most famous people in the world and I have enjoyed doing so for two reasons. One, because I want to remind myself that they are just people, like anyone else walking the face of the earth. And two, I want to be able to converse like a human being with these amazing people, and not like a star-struck, tongue-tied idiot. I sat in Gene Kelly's lap, talked with Michael Jackson, met world-renowned actors and actresses, billionaires, dancers, directors, sports superstars, politicians, and royalty. Though they all put on their pants and skirts one leg at a time, and have thoughts, pain, love, and worry, they have something I have only achieved in tiny quantities: real fame. And that's okay. It kinda has to be. I yearned badly for fame when I first moved to Los Angeles in the late '80s in pursuit of television and movie success. I became obsessed with it after seeing some of the stars' homes and the amazing cars everywhere in L.A. It took some time, but I concluded that I wasn't meant for that level of fame, and I came to a certain peace with that realization. I believe that everything happens for a reason, and what is meant to be is simply that, and that has been quite a lot.

Lucky me!

How do I think I became slightly famous? A career is about baby steps. I showed up every day and worked, and I still do. I persevered through difficult times and illness and emotional wreckage. I eventually learned to love the audience and they loved me back tenfold. I am not sure that is something you can teach a performer, but it always felt to me like the great ones had that X factor. I always wanted to be funny. I made it my mission to learn how to do that and be consistent. Being good at that has paid off in many ways.

Grandma is my vehicle to communicate the love and affection I have for the human race. They may see Grandma through their eyes, but I am lucky enough to see them as themselves. I was smart enough, with exceptions, to seize the opportunities that presented themselves to me with the help of numerous other people, and to create my own opportunities. I hope I have done so with humility and gratitude, and with much less ego than when I was new to the business. And perhaps the biggest factor in my success was my desire to be accessible to the audience. Always. Not a star in a distant galaxy, but one of them. In return, I find myself with this pretty comfortable and enjoyable level of fame.

In the season that followed my last with Big Apple Circus, I received a few wonderful mentions in New York and Boston newspaper reviews when the circus came to town with me no longer a part of it.

New York Times: "For devotees of the company, there's also a bit of sadness: this is the first year without the brilliant Barry Lubin, who retired after more than two decades as star-clown Grandma. He is missed."

Boston Globe: "Barry Lubin's Grandma is a hard act to follow."

Boston Herald: "Attending this iteration of the Big Apple Circus feels like starting over. In part, that's because beloved Grandma the Clown (Barry Lubin) has retired."

FYI: I have not retired; I have left the Big Apple Circus to pursue other lovely opportunities.

In the souvenir program book from my last season of the Big Apple Circus, I was asked to write something to the fans as a way of saying goodbye. I wrote:

One day, when you are in the audience, you may look around and see me sitting a few rows away eating popcorn and enjoying the Big Apple Circus just like you. But you will know that I secretly long to be back inside that magic ring.

I have gone back a few times, and loved seeing the circus and my friends who are still there. I have been recognized in the audience when I have visited, but not by many. I will never forget my twenty-five seasons there, and I truly miss those wonderful crowds. Those years were exquisite, joyful, magnificent, exhausting, pure fun, overwhelming, filled with love, and the greatest place any clown could ever hope to play in the entire world. I had the gig of the century. Well, a quarter century.

Ah, fame...

Men are from Mars, women are from their mothers.

Fans

I have to talk about my fans, all of whom I am very lucky to have. I even have a circus fan club in Altoona, Pennsylvania, led by one of my all-time biggest fans, David Orr. It is a chapter of Circus Fans of America called The Adam Forepaugh – Barry Lubin "Grandma" Tent. (It's a mouthful.) I have always tried to keep it simple and not play into a role for which I am not well cast. I am just a guy who worked hard, and the results of those efforts are, and always will be, unpredictable. My relationship with the fans is a big part of that journey and an unexpected pleasure. I try to get to Altoona as much as possible, and I'm occasionally booked to perform there with Royal Hanneford Circus. Whenever that happens, it always means one thing with certainty.

At Sarasota's Big Cat Habitat, being licked by a wolf, photo by Ann Hageus.

Cake!

"The Clan" is a group of fans led by their matriarch, Marion Legler, who bought the exact same thirty or so ringside seats every year at the Big Apple Circus and who cheered me on like I was the brightest shining star in the universe. I invited them backstage, always took photos with them, and was often given cookies and presents. To this day I try and keep in touch with Marion. Sometimes fans also become friends.

There is a big family of fans led by Marie Tarpey, who came to the Big Apple Circus every year. I visited at intermission whenever I knew they were in the crowd. We would always kid around, but we also shared pieces of our lives with each other. At one show, one of Marie's family members was suffering with back problems and unable to attend the circus. I asked for her cell phone and called them. Another time, I was able to brighten the day for Marie's sister, Kim, who was then suffering from a serious illness. Marie reached out to me on that occasion, and it was my honor to do a little something for her and her beautiful family. I know it can make a difference just to take a moment for someone, which is the least I can do for those people who have supported me so beautifully over the years.

A woman walked up to me as she arrived at the Big Apple Circus with her daughter and her friend. She pulled me aside and whispered to me that her daughter, who was around twelve years old and holding a Grandma doll, had been having a very rough go with her health the previous year; she had required multiple surgeries. She shared with me that her daughter had received special permission from her surgeon to bring her Grandma doll into the operating room for each operation. It was hard not to cry in that moment, and I hugged that woman and her daughter probably a little too hard that day. I wonder what has become of them.

There are countless kind and wonderful people who have told me that they had a Grandma doll on their bed or on their mantle, or that they had a photo of me with their family on their refrigerator, or as that year's Christmas card. In their way, they had brought me into their homes, which is a great honor.

Geraldine Ferraro, one-time Vice-Presidential candidate, asked me to be the centerpiece of her family Christmas card one year. As we were about to shoot I asked, "Are you sure you want a Jewish transvestite clown on your family Christmas card?" After staring at me for a rather uncomfortably long time, she said, "Yes," and we shot it during intermission. I would love to see that one now.

I have to say that it is rare when I socialize with fans outside of the workplace, but I have two lovely "stalkers" who are the nicest people in the world: Linda and Andy. When I get an invite to socialize with fans, I usually decline, using an excuse of some sort, because I do not actually know them, and I'm not that social of a person. I am kind of shy in real life. In a way it is the opposite of how I present Grandma as being accessible. Maybe my fans get a mixed message. After the show ends, the lights fade, the makeup comes off, I go back to just being me. But with Linda and Andy, and there are others, I can be myself. If I lived closer, I would surely hang out with them more. They have been to an unreasonably large number of my performances and Linda admits to being a bit obsessed. They brought me food at one show, enough for the entire weekend. Cupcakes another. They go to see lots of other circuses and shows, so they aren't two recluses who emerge just to see only me. Whenever they visit, I try to have a meal with them, even if it is in makeup and costume between shows. There are some people who are so special you just want to spend as much time with them as possible, even if they are "stalkers." That's Linda and Andy.

I have had countless conversations during intermission of the Big Apple Circus where I went out into the audience during the pause and sat down and just talked with the people next to me. Often times these experiences were lovely, funny, fun, and at times, unexpectedly emotional. I don't know why so many people opened up to me during those occasions, but I also opened up to them. I was sitting on an airplane awaiting takeoff in Oslo, Norway, when a young woman leaned over and said, "I hope you don't take this the wrong way, but are you a clown?" I answered yes. "Are you Grandma?" she asked, and I answered yes again. She told me that she was a very big fan, and that I had even spoken several times over the years to her and her mom and family. We became friends instantly on that plane, but it seems we had become friends before in other circumstances. Funny, isn't it? People feel like they know me through Grandma. I suppose it would be hard to argue with that.

A long time ago, while working in the audience with Ringling Brothers and Barnum & Bailey Circus, I realized that I wanted Grandma to be accessible to the audience – to let them know I was one of them – that I was just as in awe as they were of the atmosphere, the artists, the performance. I never wanted to play the role of "the star" – above the audience, in need of their awe, asking them to treat me differently. Accessibility is one reason I seem to have been able to touch so many lives, and in turn they have touched mine.

At a certain point years ago, without planning to, my attitude changed from clowning for love, attention, respect, and money, to simply going out there and loving the audience. The results were interesting, especially because I didn't specifically intend for this to occur. To go out in front of the audience with that agenda of "what's in it for me?" can certainly work, and work well on certain levels. I got results for sure. The changeover to simply going out there for the honor of performing for people, and the desire I felt to simply love the crowd – well, that was life-altering, and career-altering. I am not a selfless and completely giving person by nature, to be honest, so it was a change. All I can tell you is: the audience gave me back tenfold whatever love I gave to them. Powerful.

"Soggy Guy" from New Jersey wrote me a letter telling me that his daughter had been suffering greatly from illness, and how badly the family was suffering along with her. He told me how the simple random act of me bringing him into the circus ring had made her so happy, laughing at her dad getting into a water spitting fight with Grandma, and how that had meant so much to him and his daughter and the entire family to share that experience. It was pure luck that I picked him. And I wonder how they are now. I still have the letter.

To all the people, young and old, who made me feel like a part of your lives and your family's lives, I can't thank you enough. I simply went out there and performed for you and tried to give you my love in the form of doing silly little things in my silly little character in the red dress and gray wig. You embraced me with love in return, and this overwhelms me...as I sit quietly, in a kitchen in Stockholm, writing this to you now.

A wise man once said, I hope you like my potato chips.

Baby You Can Drive My Grandma

Grandma, as amazing as she is, can't be in more than one place at a time. Over the years, there have been situations where I had to turn down appearances because I was already booked. Then, as she became a bigger star and diva of epic proportions, the demand for her was more than one man in a red dress and gray wig could handle. Therefore, cloning needed to happen…in the form of licensing.

Clown cloning.

There have been several others who have shared my spotlight by wearing the red dress and gray wig over the years. My ex-wife played Grandma beautifully for three weeks when I had chicken pox in the summer of 1991. Jimmy and Tisha Tinsman, married multi-talented acrobats and comedians, put on my makeup and costume as practical jokes in early Big Apple Circus days in the mid 1980s. But licensing was a new concept for me, and one that brought great criticism from people I loved and respected, along with a lot of other interesting reactions.

At Paul Binder's suggestion, I started to license Grandma in 2001. I left the circus in 1998 to pursue other opportunities, but he and I started talking about my coming back to the Big Apple Circus for the 2001 season and we talked about a multi-year contract. He was hoping that we could work together on something mutually beneficial and long-term for the circus and me, with a much longer commitment than I had ever considered before. I told him I wanted to perform in New York City, but didn't want to go on the tour anywhere other than to my beloved Boston. He hatched the idea to license Grandma so we could both have our cake and eat it, too. That way, I could do the gigs I wanted, and the ones I couldn't or didn't want to do, Grandma could still be there. I would cast, train, and maintain another performer to play Grandma. After lots of discussion, I signed a deal for five years, with options to extend. It gave me security for my family, peace of mind, and a great place to work.

The licensing deal was unique in the company. The circus was founded and set up as a not-for-profit corporation, much like a ballet or opera company. I was set up as a for-profit show business entity. Sometimes those two philosophies clashed. This was my job, after all, so of course I wanted to make as much money as I could to support my family. The company didn't operate that way, with the concept of profit nearly against the principals of the institution. They are an institution, and I was just an inmate. For the most part, under the direction of my business manager, then General Manager of the circus, Guillaume Dufresnoy, it was a great deal for all of us.

I do love this photo! Circus Krone 2007. Photo by Liam Kreal

The circus signed me long-term so they could build their brand around my character. And I was very good at talking about the circus at every opportunity and being available for any and all media events as a means to promote myself, and therefore, the circus. Some feathers were ruffled by my personality and character being everywhere, but that is what the organization wanted and chose freely. I cherished the opportunity to do so, and had two great people behind the publicity machine to promote me everywhere possible: Joel Dein, the Director of Communications, and Phil Thurston, the Public Relations manager.

TV commercials, newspapers, magazine ads, the sides of buses, feature articles, subway ads, a banner with my image in front of Lincoln Center and on the street by Government Center in Boston…Grandma was suddenly everywhere. They even arranged to have a street named after me: "Grandma Way" in Boston. Talk about an honor! There was a City Hall ceremony and official unveiling. THAT was cool! I threw out the first pitch at a major league baseball game, rang the opening AND closing bells of the New York Stock Exchange, lit the top of the Empire State Building, and so much more. I was on the side of milk cartons (though that prompted some kids to believe I was missing – no kidding). I was one of the five clowns interviewed by a woman from the Wall Street Journal for a feature called "The Power Clowns." Her angle, we thought, was to reveal how important the clown had become recently to the North American circus business. We were all honored and excited to participate. Instead, she made us all sound like greedy bastards. Not fun. In my case, she incorrectly stated that the Big Apple Circus had to accept my terms because the circus needed my character. Not true. They say that any publicity is good publicity. Let's agree to disagree. Regardless, Grandma was everywhere because of that licensing deal.

At first, licensing Grandma simply meant that I would play the character for part of the year, and cast, train, and rehearse another person to play Grandma for the remainder of the circus tour. As it actually worked out, I rehearsed the show in upstate New York, opened the show in Virginia, played nearly all of the shows in those two places, and handed it off to the other Grandma in Georgia that February. The first few months of the tour, I rehearsed the acts with the licensee, had them sit and watch several shows, and then they did a few shows with me in the audience taking notes. When the show rehearsed in Atlanta in February each year, a few weeks after closing in New York, I would put them into the show full-time, giving notes through the opening weekend, and then I was gone. They generally performed around twenty weeks of shows until the tour ended in late July.

I also found, at various times – when things were a little slow in New Jersey – that I longed to hit the road and play a show or two in the circus. So I did. It was so much fun to just pop in, always with permission, and perform. In Boston, it was always much more than a show or two, because I loved being there so much. I had lived there for seven years, and it felt like my second home.

These talented people played the character so beautifully that the audience treated me like it had been me all along playing their city whenever I popped in to do a show. In other words, I would step into the show in a market that I had rarely personally played since 1998 and they welcomed Grandma passionately. Most people probably didn't know it wasn't always me, though we never hid that fact. That meant that Mark Gindick, Matthew Pauli, Josh Matthews, and Mike Garner (aka "Korean Grandma") were all doing great jobs. I watched each of them perform the role, and often laughed my ass off. In fact, I occasionally felt a tinge of jealousy when audiences laughed at, applauded, and loved Grandma when it wasn't me in that ring. A good result, I would say.

It made me happy that my creation, in addition to bringing audiences laughs, brought employment and income to others. There were days when four Grandmas were working at the same time on three continents. That still blows my mind. It was surreal when the licensee would come up with a great idea for Grandma and then when I performed the show the next time, I would ask them for permission to use that new material. Sometimes it was a whole routine, sometimes a little sight gag, sometimes a sweet moment. Though they always said yes,

Grandma in Monte Carlo. Photo by Danielle Lubin

I never wanted to step on their creative toes. The answer they gave was that they would be honored, but it was really my honor and my pleasure. That is what happens when you hire really talented and creative people.

With pimping out Grandma, only one licensee deal was a disaster, but I credit the producer with screwing that one up. Making the deal was a no brainer: thirty-eight weeks in a very nice hotel theater in Seoul, South Korea. I would like to have gone there to install "Korean Grandma" Mike Garner, but my schedule wouldn't allow it. We rehearsed the character and routines at Lincoln Center, which also gave Mike a great opportunity to watch my Grandma at work.

I cast Mike for a few very good reasons: he was very funny, he was Korean, and he would probably have no trouble lasting, and actually enjoying, a nearly year-long run so far from home. He was interested in researching his roots and he was thrilled with this offer. Unlike any other licensee, Mike was a foot taller than me and weighed fifty pounds more, but he was a very funny man. The producer understood exactly who he was getting and accepted the casting choice with open arms. Little did I know, to Mike's great disadvantage, that the producer wanted to do a Cirque du Soleil style show in Seoul. Grandma doesn't really fit naturally into that style of entertainment.

Mike tried very hard to listen to mostly unreasonable directions about the character and material, and was doomed to fail from the start. I would have failed, too, if it had been me there. Mike lasted nine days in Korea. I felt terrible for him, but he was a real gentleman about it. He had sold his car and given up his apartment in Atlanta, and taken all his possessions to his parent's house in Georgia. Two weeks later he was homeless, carless, and none too happy. The producer screwed him, and had even refused to pay his airfare back to the U.S., even though the contract required him to. Adding to that, he tried to charge Mike for the days in the hotel he was forced to stay in before the flight departed Korea. The circus paid for him to come back. Later, in a great return of the favor he did for us in Korea, especially because it didn't work out, Mike was hired by the Big Apple Circus to perform – not as Grandma, but as his own unique clown, in the sixteen-month-long "Circus" tour with Britney Spears. He traveled all over the world, made a good living, and he loved it!

Matthew Pauli played Grandma for six seasons and did a fantastic job. The thing I found out quickly about Matt in rehearsals, which I didn't realize in the audition, was that the man could not spit water. That may not be important for a lot of professions, but this gig was different. I tried to teach him, but I have found over the years that some people just don't have the correct embouchure to play the trumpet, and it applies to water spitting as well. I teach various alternatives when the person reveals that they cannot spit water in a small stream for a bit of a distance and time. The act was "Singin' in the Rain" with Mark Gindick, and was designed to take advantage of Mark's dancing ability and Grandma's water spitting prowess to provide the "rain." Matt came up with an alternative, which I ended up using. He took a big plastic water bottle that you could

Shpritz anyone? Photo by Paul Gutheil

squeeze, and on cue he shot a helluva great stream on Mark, which got a much bigger laugh than my water spitting ever did. When I did the shows after Matt perfected it, I did it that way.

Matt was also challenged by an act I created that required he play a full drum set mounted on wheels. I don't play the drums, but I found a way to make it fun and funny. Matt had a lot of trouble at first until I gave him one important direction: "suck big." Yes, that was my direction, the intention being to get him playing hard and fast and not worrying about the results. He then proceeded to whale on the drums. It was startling, really. The audience went NUTS. He was simply committing to slamming drums and cymbals with sticks with no concern for accuracy, rhythm, or beat. He kicked ass. He kicked ass so well that when I went into a show after watching Matt do one, I tried to do what he did and failed miserably. The audience simply looked at me. I was unable to suck big. Maybe I am a better director than drummer.

Each week that the licensee performed in the Big Apple Circus, I was paid a licensing fee by the show. And there were other occasions outside the ring besides Korea where deals were made. Circuses, theaters, corporate engagements, fashion shows, television shows, private performances. In each case, I was paid a fee, which was split with the circus. There is an expression for this in show business: making money in your sleep – a term I rather like.

My deal with the circus also included pursuing other business opportunities while away from the tour, in exchange for "a piece of the action." That was more or less six months out of the year. In theory, I could sit on my ass for six months and do nothing and collect a paycheck, but I was much more ambitious than that. During two of those years, I teamed up with Yvette Kaplan and created television shows for the television network Nickelodeon. Yvette was a very successful and highly regarded talent in the world of animation, as well as a great partner. Together, we were creators, executive producers, and I was the star of two pilots – Oops and Daisy, and Oops Makes the Bed – both financed with Nickelodeon money. Oops was my character, a lovable, bumbling handyman playing opposite an adorable ballerina. We also developed three other concepts for Nickelodeon. For one very exciting moment, we received the "green light" to go into production on Oops and Daisy. We hired a production team and started to build a shoot schedule for the first season of twenty shows. As often happens in show business, it never happened. But it was a great opportunity and really great fun working with a treasure like Yvette. In the animation world, Yvette is a goddess.

During the off-times from circus touring, I would pursue live and TV gigs, both in the U.S. and abroad. I performed in New Zealand, Germany, Austria, Hungary, Monaco, directed a performer in the South Pacific, taught in various parts of the world, and the experiences were nearly all positive. Well, not 100% positive regarding licensing the character. Though I felt great about giving lots of employment to my licensees from 2001 until 2013, both in and out the Big Apple Circus ring, some people who I respect enormously found that "selling Grandma" this way was just not a good thing. They weren't jealous. Their point was: Grandma was Barry Lubin. They couldn't understand how I could do this and felt that it bordered on unethical. My rationale was that it paid my bills nicely, paid the bills of those four other people nicely, and actually enabled the character to bring pleasure in shows on four continents simultaneously. The very popular Blue Man Group licensed their work, as did Slava's Snowshow, a clown show that was created by and starred a wonderful Russian clown, Slava Polunin. The originators rarely played those parts anymore. That is simply good show business, emphasis on "business."

At times, people came to see Grandma in a show expecting it to be me, though I was actually elsewhere in the world. A big circus producer and friend came to see the Big Apple Circus, and when Grandma kept ignoring him as "she" passed by him repeatedly without saying hello during the performance, he became quite irritated with "me." He was blown away when he found out it wasn't me; the licensee was so good that he couldn't tell it wasn't me. That same producer has been generous enough to hire my licensees and me several times since then.

I was told, and smartly so, when I cast and trained the other Grandmas, that I shouldn't expect them to be just like me. The producer said think of it in terms of "Grandma 1a" – it will be a different incarnation of the character, based on my work, but never the same, because they would inevitably interpret Grandma their own way. I always felt myself doing a balancing act when training the other Grandmas, because if they were going into an existing show, they needed to fulfill what was expected of them by that show. In a new show, there was leeway to be more creative, and in a city where Grandma was unknown, nearly total freedom to perform in any way that they saw fit, as long as it was clean, worked well, and got the laughs.

Mark Gindick was the first licensee, and frankly, his start was pretty rough. So rough, in fact, that I thought this whole experiment was going to be a failure. There were a couple of people who asked for their money back at the box office, and a few sent letters to the Big Apple Circus complaining about Grandma not being me or having had a bad day. It only took two shows to correct it, and Mark became my go-to guy, doing many engagements for me both in the Big Apple Circus and for other producers. Mark quickly learned how to make the character his own, and the more he played Grandma, the better and more comfortable he became. To me, it is my life's work. To Mark, it is a gig, and rightly so. Mark has his own shows in development and many other talents, but this provides him with income and a certain amount of fun, I hope. He and I happen to love the circus and clowning. As Mark's mother once said to me, "Are you going to hire Mark for any more Grandma gigs? He does 'you' better than you."

It ripped my guts out when Dmitri, the legendary Swiss clown, complained to me about my business choice. I always found myself apologizing to Dmitri. On the other hand, Cirque Du Soleil and Disney, among others, have had enormous success putting other players into roles originally created by great performers. When you go to Disney World, there isn't just one trained Mickey Mouse. Broadway does it successfully all the time. I will say this: licensing Grandma was the best business move I have ever made in my career. The licensees have been excellent, we all made money, and the standard of the character was never compromised. I get to play Grandma whenever I want, and I also get to pick and choose which gig I want to perform when there are two or more offers on the table during the same time period. Sounds like good business to me. Besides, why wouldn't I want to see something I created succeed, flourish, and make lots of people happy? Sounds win-win to me. I will happily continue to pursue other licensing deals.

> Dare to be different, even if it means conforming and doing totally unoriginal stuff.

Anecdotes, Near Death Experiences, and Ring of Fame

I'd like to take some time now to tell you some stories that don't necessary fit together with any connective tissue, but that I feel are worth telling because, well, just because I wanna:

The Big Apple Circus box office manager, Ann Foley, told me this story:

A father called the box office today and told me that his mother had just died, and he had to tell his four-year-old daughter that Grandma had passed away. He broke the news to her as gently as he could. She cried and cried and finally calmed down enough to ask, "Daddy, does this mean we can't go to the Big Apple Circus anymore?"

I dragged New York Yankees legend Derek Jeter around the Big Apple Circus ring as he sat on a drum set mounted on wheels. Me, a small man in drag, pulling the Yankees Captain around a circus ring like a ragdoll. Later that year, at a game at Yankee Stadium, I sat with a friend and posed the question, "How many people, out of the fifty-five thousand fans at this game, do you think have ever dragged Derek Jeter around a circus ring on a drum set mounted on wheels?"

His guess:

"One."

I'm pretty sure he was correct. If not, that would be very weird. Being a die-hard Yankees fan, that moment was one of the great thrills of my life.

In the spring of 1996, I was invited to a pre-autograph

session buffet at the Florida State Fair with the New York Yankees following their World Series victory. There were just three of us besides the players and manager, which included myself and the friends who got me the invite, Monica and Johnny Welde, of "Welde's Bears" fame. I went dressed as Grandma, because I was appearing in a circus at the fair, of which Yankee owner, George Steinbrenner, was the chairman. Mr. Steinbrenner was a big fan of the Weldes and sponsored their bear act, and in exchange, the Weldes had their bears wearing Yankees uniforms and walking on rolling globes that looked like giant Yankees baseballs. The Yankees were generally amused by Grandma and were very accessible and generous, with the exception of one of my heroes, whose name shall remain unknown. When I asked for his autograph, he snubbed me. I was truly hurt by this, but it taught me a great lesson: never turn down a request for a moment of my time, whether it's for an autograph or a handshake or just a little hello. That one tiny moment can mean so much to the person on the receiving end, and it can hurt so much if you don't give them that moment.

I got to throw out the first pitch at a Major League baseball game in Detroit. It was a promotion for the Big Apple Circus, which was playing near the stadium, and this was something I had always dreamed of doing. When it was time, I ran out to the mound, dust-busted the rubber on top of the mound, and threw a pitch low and outside to the Detroit Tigers catcher, Chad Kreuter. He ran over to me smiling, shook my hand, autographed the baseball, and handed it back to me. The crowd only clapped a little, but I loved every moment.

I worked several circus engagements with Becky Kimes as my Ringmistress. Becky was a gorgeous blonde and the polar opposite to the pedestrian looking Grandma. I loved to crack her up, and there were times when she was laughing so hard at something stupid I did in the ring that it literally did stop the show. The audience often fell apart laughing at Becky laughing at me, so I didn't feel too badly when it happened, and it happened A LOT! On one occasion, near the end of an engagement, Becky and I chose to play a little prank on the cast and crew, which backfired quite badly. She had a large number of long blond "falls" – attachable hair-lengthening wigs which matched her own hair – and when she told me she was about to throw one out, we hatched our plan. Showtime.

I sneaked into the ring as Becky was making an announcement in the middle of the show, and I pulled out a pair of scissors, made sure everyone in the audience could see, and cut about two feet off the length of her hair. She'd made it look like she had no idea it was happening. The cast was horrified. Worse than that, the audience wanted to kill me for butchering her "beautiful hair." I was literally booed out of the circus ring by thousands in attendance that day. Naturally, Becky cracked up once again, but as far as the audience was concerned, the damage was done. I wanted to crawl under a rock and stay there until that show ended and the audience left, but I had several more appearances to make. I made them as professionally as possible, but I can't recall having a worse feeling during a performance in my entire career.

For a few months in early 1978, I worked at the now-defunct Florida theme park "Circus World." I loved it there and was cast in the one-ring circus show inside an air-conditioned building, which was a welcome change from the heat of central Florida. I was in the opening production number and chose a unique way to be noticed: by being seemingly dragging on my stomach while holding onto the back of a circus wagon. There was a large skateboard under me, which the audience couldn't see, so the effect was a good one, and it led to a lot of laughs. One day, I was dragging on my stomach and I heard a growing roar from the audience unlike anything I had heard before, and it was getting louder and louder. I couldn't really check it out since I was lying on my stomach on a skateboard behind a big wagon. It seems that one of the elephants ahead of me in the opening parade had done what elephants do when nature calls – in this case, both number one and number two. As I got closer and closer to impending disaster, the rising audience noise became deafening. Finally, there was an explosion, as I got one of the biggest laughs of my career playing the incomparable role of "The Human Mop."
Ain't show biz great?

Dick Monday and I worked at Disneyland in California for a special event called Circus Fantasy at Disneyland. It was held during a traditionally slow time of the year to boost ticket sales, January through March, from 1986 to 1988. There were shows and strolling clowns and a circus parade and much more. After being a part of a successful variety show at Circus Fantasy during that first year, Dick and I were offered a small stage to perform on at a place known as "Coke Corner," located on Main Street U.S.A. Coke Corner was a food concession area with tables, and a stage was added just for our show. On the first day, management spoke very sternly to us and said, "If you affect the sale of one soda or one hot dog, you are out of there." A bit stunned, we didn't really know what to do other than proceed with our three daily clown shows as planned.

They didn't want to give us a microphone, afraid that the noise might affect the sale of one soda or one hot dog. Absurdist that he is, Dick mounted a megaphone on a microphone stand and called it a "megraphone." After one day, management relented and gave us microphones. At Coke Corner was one of Disneyland's favorite entertainers, Rod, who for over twenty years had regaled the crowds with his clever piano playing and friendly banter. When we moved into his territory, and he was informed that he had to accompany our shows, he became one pissed-off piano player. We thought we were in trouble, but within a few days, Rod became a great friend and ally and loved the variety that our shows provided him, because not one of our performances was ever the same.

There were usually so few people in the park for our first show at 10:00 a.m. that we did what we called "The Morning Show." We just casually bantered with Rod and the audience, and had a blast improvising each morning. The looseness of that show made it our favorite of the day quite often. Ironically, on the final day of our eight-week engagement, management came back to look at what we were doing and freaked out. They said, "If we had known you were improvising shows at Disneyland, we would have stopped you long ago."

Once, during "The Morning Show," Dick and I were getting bigger laughs than usual, and didn't know why until I'd turned around and saw that Disney characters, Chip & Dale, were upstaging us. When I busted them, they ran off. I was so pissed off that I tore ass across Disneyland in my Grandma costume at top speed running after Chip (maybe it was Dale), who was just about backstage by the time I reached them. The sight of me sprinting at top speed across Disneyland as Grandma and then tearing Chip a new one (or maybe Dale), must have been shocking to anyone who witnessed my unreasonably wild tirade against this beloved Disney character. Inside the costume was a teenage girl who just wanted to have some fun with the clowns. I had to be restrained.

Dick chose to play his hobo character for the first year at Circus Fantasy and created the most brilliant ride on Main Street U.S.A. He lay down by the curb on this famous street at the entrance to Disneyland and offered any passerby the opportunity to go on Disney's latest attraction, "The Gutter Ride." There must be ten thousand people who still have photos of themselves lying next to this beloved bum at Disneyland.
Genius.

On another baseball promotion, when the Big Apple Circus was in Boston, I got to go onto the field at Fenway Park. I asked the P.R. person from the Red Sox if I could run into left field and crash into the famous Green Monster and fall down. (The Monster is the legendary high wall that dominates left field.) He let me. How many clowns in red dresses and gray wigs do you think have ever run into the Green Monster in the history of Fenway Park?

I am researching this question and will get back to you shortly.

I was hired to be the half-time entertainment at the Boston Garden for a Celtics basketball game. I did my giant hula-hoop act. The half-time crowd could not have been less responsive. In retrospect, maybe I should have worn a bikini and had fire shooting out of my ass to stand a better chance at success. The part I liked best was that I had to come in early to rehearse and the P.R. woman let us (me and my Big Apple Circus P.R. guy, Phil Thurston) shoot some baskets on the famous parquet floor. For some reason, I couldn't dunk the ball that day.

A wonderful supporter and friend of the Big Apple Circus was Raleigh Cox. She was on the Board of Directors and had always treated me like family. She passed away after a long illness, and her children, whom I had known since they were little, asked me to come to Raleigh's memorial service at the Cathedral of St. John the Divine in New York. I told them I would be honored to attend, and asked them if they wanted me to come as myself or as Grandma, whom Raleigh had always gotten a big kick out of. They left it up to me and said, "We want you to come because our mom loved you. Do what you think she would have wanted." I came to her memorial service dressed as Grandma, which I believe is what Raleigh would have wanted, to help celebrate her wonderful life.

Father Jerry Hogan was the circus chaplain, a job he loved

and embraced because he had been a fan of the circus since he was a kid. He performed weddings, funerals, baptisms, and blessed the tents of many circuses before they began their tour, including the Big Apple Circus. It was a non-denominational blessing, and I never failed to attend. Father Jerry was also there to counsel anyone in need for any reason, and I often shared with him my troubles and worries. When the circus was in Boston near his home parish, he asked me to come to Sunday mass to help him deliver his sermon on the subject of respect. His flock had come to expect some unique services and guests whenever there was a circus nearby. The idea was that Father Jerry would speak from the pulpit about respecting the elderly, and suddenly Grandma would appear and lip-sync to Aretha Franklin's "Respect." Just before this rather unique performance experience, I asked Father Hogan, "Are you sure you want a Jewish transvestite in your sermon?" He answered without hesitation. "Absolutely!"
It was a hit.
Praise the Lord!
(Literally.)

I was asked to appear as Grandma at a charity event for a member of the Big Apple Circus Board of Directors, Ruth Schumann. Ruth was a friend of then-Mayor Michael Bloomberg of the great city of New York, and I was told he would be coming to the event to speak. His Honor was a very important member of the circus' Board of Directors before he became the mayor, and I had met and spoken to him numerous times. I was walking around entertaining people in the crowd at Ruth's event when the mayor's advance woman and several other very serious large people arrived and quickly surveyed the room. She walked directly up to me and, nearly yelling at me, barked, "Move...NOW!" I obediently stepped aside for the entrance of the mayor. He was announced and walked into the ballroom along with his security team. Naturally all eyes were on His Honor as he entered, and just when he was about to pass by, he spotted me standing obediently against the wall (I am hard to miss). He walked directly over to me and we talked for about five minutes, with all eyes in the room of over five hundred people upon us. We were joking around pretty much the same as when he came to the Big Apple Circus. I could imagine what people there must have been thinking: "Who the hell is that clown the mayor is talking to?" He finally excused himself and walked up the podium, where he spoke for ten minutes in support of Ms. Schumann's charity. He left the stage and walked right back over to me. We talked for another few minutes and then he exited the building. He spoke to no one else, including the host of the event. Just me.

Thrilled? You bet I was.

I rang the closing bell at the New York Stock Exchange. That was cool as hell, plus it was broadcast worldwide each day on the financial networks. We had to walk through the trading floor on the way to the bell ringing as business was in full swing. It was like being on Mars…with countless wires and monitors and very aggressive men and women doing their bidding. The waiting room upstairs from the exchange was a secure room with guards everywhere – a place where leaders of business, sports, and politics had sat before ringing the same bell I was about to ring. Presidents had sat in that room. Now a man in a dress sat there. When it was time, we headed to the bell ceremony, which was on a small balcony overlooking the trading floor. As I rang the closing bell and everyone clapped as they always do, the president of the New York Stock Exchange whispered to me that I had just stopped over a trillion dollars of stocks from trading. I quickly looked around on the floor, just in case someone had accidentally dropped a million dollars or so. They wouldn't really miss it, would they? Then I wondered: if I had hit the bell one more time, would they start trading again?

My face was on the poster of the Big Apple Circus quite often. I was in The New York Times every day in the ad for the circus. I was in the television commercials running all the time in New York and in the other markets we played. My image was on the sides of buses and inside subways. In December of one season, I was burnt out from the long run of shows and was admittedly "phoning in" my performances during the heavy holiday schedule. I went to see the Broadway musical "42nd Street" with my daughters one night after doing two early circus shows. Onstage were a hundred dancers working their asses off for the entertainment of the audience. Not one of them was on the poster, on the sides of buses, in The New York Times every day, but they were giving 110% of themselves for our pleasure. It was then that I was determined I would never again half-ass a performance, knowing it would take very little effort to truly give 100% of myself each and every time I was performing.

From that day on, I never phoned in another performance.

When I was working in the audience in my Ringling days, improvising and learning who Grandma was, I stood on the armrests of a seat and sat down sideways on a random man's shoulder, first placing a pillow there.

Ipanema Beach, Rio, Brazil. Photo by MF Hoh.

Though I didn't place any weight on the man, he picked me up and threw me. I landed four rows away. Fortunately I wasn't hurt, nor was anyone else. It made me realize that while I am working in the audience, I am in their world. I learned to be more careful, but I was shaking for quite a while after that little incident.

During my first season in Ringling in 1975, I was working as Grandma in the audience at Madison Square Garden before the show. I was suddenly surrounded by eight giggling teenage girls who started to push me around a bit. I tried to turn this into something entertaining, but I quickly realized that they were actually trying to push me down the stairs. (There are a lot of stairs at Madison Square Garden.) I learned that when your life is in jeopardy, comedy and circus be damned. RUN!

During the year that I dropped out of Emerson College and auditioned for Clown College, I had a job as a bill collector. I called people all day to try to collect overdue bills from utilities, hospitals, doctors, banks, and many other businesses. The desks at my office handled debtors by the letters of their last name, and I had the Ms and part of the Ns. I had let my New England Telephone bill go unpaid, and three months later it was coming to my office for collection. I never explained why, but I asked my supervisor if I could change with the person handling the Ls. He had no problem with that and neither did the person handling the Ls. My phone bill came in to my desk, I paid it, and earned the 33% commission off myself.

I dropped a prop box from a Ringling production number on my foot in Anaheim, California. The top of my foot swelled up, but I was able to walk on it just fine and work without pain. My costume for the production number included a tight jazz boot, and it just wouldn't fit, but I was willing to work, anyway. The boss clown took one look at my swollen foot and sent me home. I protested that I really wasn't in any pain, but he sent me away. I called a friend of mine, a lovely blonde who owned a lovely red Mustang convertible, and she brought along her lovely blond friend. In view of the entire clown alley, one on each arm, they "helped me" into the top-down convertible, and off we went to the beach for the weekend.

Accidents happen.

I was sitting on railroad tracks next to the circus train late one night smoking a joint with a fellow clown. Obviously, the Ringling train had to park on train tracks, and sometimes, next to the train, there were active train-line tracks known as The Main Line. We were getting pretty toasted when we heard a very loud train horn sounding. The intense lights from the engine were blinding us, and I suddenly realized a train was heading right at us. The engineer was sounding a warning, but for a moment we were like deer frozen in those headlights. I grabbed my friend and pulled him off the tracks just as the train went by, and didn't realize until later what had nearly happened.

We were that stoned.

Good shit can lead to bad shit.

I almost died a few other times. I was a Boy Scout hiking on a narrow trail that hugged the side of a mountain in New Mexico, and I was too lazy to roll my sleeping bag properly. This caused me to fall off the mountain when the trail became very narrow and a rock jutted out and made contact with my impossibly wide sleeping bag, which was sticking out too far from my backpack. Off I went. It was about a thousand-foot drop, but a few feet down, a tree was growing sideways off the side of the mountain and I caught it. I was last in line on the hike because I was kind of a pain in the ass to everyone. From the tree just below the trail, I called out for help and the next to last person was able to assist me and pulled me back up onto the trail and we continued on. Afterwards, I tried to explain what had happened to the rest of the Boy Scout troupe and the scoutmaster, but no one believed me.

I had a surfing accident when I was in my teens. While I was riding a pretty big wave, I wiped out. I fought to reach the surface in the churning white water, but the moment I came up for air, another big wave hit me in the face and I nearly drowned. I was saved by a nearby surfer who safely brought me to shore. I quit surfing that afternoon, but I might try it again some day.

Surf happens.

The Ringling Circus train stopped very early one morning on a run from Los Angeles to Northern California. I was standing on the vestibule watching America go by. (The vestibule is where passengers get on and off the train cars.) I didn't know why we were stopped, but I spotted a very comfortable looking folding beach chair in a nearby backyard, and I thought it would be much more comfortable sitting on that than standing for hours on the vestibule. I got off the circus train, crossed another set of tracks, and heard a train horn off in the distance. As I approached the scene of the near-crime, a very nice woman came outside to look at the spectacle of the circus train more or less in her backyard. Luckily, I hadn't yet reached the object of my desire. We started to chat and she told me that we were in Santa Barbara. She never knew what my true intentions were. A train then came speeding through on the track I had just crossed, which was traveling between the circus train and us. I realized that the circus train had moved onto a sidetrack to allow this other train to pass us. Just then, the circus train started slowly moving. I thought I might have to find another way to get to Northern California unless matters changed and quickly. The circus train was picking up speed, and finally this very long freight train passed. The track was clear and I ran like hell and caught up to my open vestibule – the only place I could have possibly hopped back onto the train. As I waved goodbye to this very nice woman, I felt more than a little pang of guilt.

The Big Apple Circus traveled to Philadelphia to play in a park opposite the Philadelphia Art Museum. As we pulled into the park with our trailer, I noticed a homeless woman asleep on a park bench covered by cardboard. She was oblivious to what was happening all around her. After two or three hours of set-up, she finally awoke. I will never forget the look on her face. The first look was one of wonder and awe as she looked around. A moment later, the look was one of profound sadness as she realized that her "home" was no longer her home. She slowly gathered her belongings and walked off. I wondered if perhaps the old woman had run away from home, and now her home was taken over by a band of people who, in their own way, had run away from home. I wrote a screenplay and a theatrical play based on that experience; the film, as of this writing, is in pre-production.

I was walking along the ring curb in spotlights during a performance of Big Apple Circus when a beautiful woman, who was sitting in the front row, said to me, "I sleep with you every night." Stunned, I just stopped and looked at her, all fifteen hundred audience members looking at me looking at her. I processed a number of inappropriate responses, wisely chose not to say any of them, and continued on to the spot where I did my clown bit, and exited the ring. The moment intermission began, I walked over to her and said, "What?" She told me that she had purchased a Grandma doll from the circus concessions stand, it was in her bed, and she slept with it every night.

Dang…

The Big Apple Circus was doing an engagement in Detroit, and for promotion I appeared as Grandma at a nearby mall. Apparently there was a transvestite convention in town. Two men, dressed to the nines as women, passed me. They looked me up and down and one said, "Oh, that's interesting," as if this were my personal choice for the transvestite convention.

Over the course of several seasons with the Big Apple Circus, the trio of Michael Christensen, Jeff Gordon, and I performed many audience participation routines. Often the volunteer would be a random child chosen from the crowd, and on one occasion we chose a young boy of about nine for our clown routine. He went through the paces very well and helped provide great laughs for the audience, never at his expense. He took a bow to great applause and went back to his seat. The following day, we received a note from his mother explaining that her son was severely autistic, and that his brief time in the ring was the first time in his entire life that he had ever truly connected with anyone outside his family. There wasn't a dry eye in clown alley that day.

A woman walked up to me with her two-year-old son at the Big Apple Circus and she was very excited. She said, "Joey here wants to be just like you when he grows up!" I looked at Joey and said, "So let me get this straight, Joey. When you grow up, you want to be a bitter 55-year-old bloated Jewish man with a receding hairline who wears a dress?" He just looked at me. Thank GOD his mom laughed.

When I was a First-of-May clown on Ringling, I became friends with the Polish teeterboard and trampoline troupes. I was half-Polish, so it seemed natural, and they were great folks... except on train runs from one town to the next. I couldn't pass through the Polish train car without being pulled into one of their rooms and more or less forced to drink vodka or whiskey with them. I had to learn how to scoot super-fast through their car, because whatever they were drinking never agreed with me. And that is saying something, coming from a man who had an addiction problem at the time. Hmm, still do, actually.

I enjoyed wandering up into the audience in the big arenas that Ringling played on their tours. I had such a good time using these places as my own playground and discovered so many things, and even entertained people while learning. I also liked to test the audience. One way I did this was to walk slowly up the stairs, which would often take five or ten minutes of climbing to get the top of the section. Then I would just as slowly roll down the stairs. It was very slow, very controlled. People would see this little old lady "falling" down the steps and many times they would leap from their aisle seats to my rescue. They would carefully help me up, but then see my clown makeup.

I am not kidding when I tell you that, 100% of the time, they dropped me once they saw my face.

Sometimes I would go all the way up to the worst seats in the arena during the pre-show, usually upper balcony all the way to the side. It was like sitting in the worst seats at a football game. I found that when I visited those people, they absolutely loved it. They never expected to get any attention so far from the arena floor. They were so pleased just to be noticed, and they often barely had enough money to afford seeing the show with their families. I entertained them for a while, and then conspired with them. I told them that when I was on the arena floor during the show, I was going to look over at them and wave, probably from the farthest opposite corner. When I did, I asked them to cheer as loud as they could. Then I left. The show would begin, and any time I looked over and waved, the entire section of several hundred people would erupt like I had just scored a touchdown. The effect was two-fold. First, the entire audience looked over to that section wondering what the hell was going on. At the same time, the entire cast and crew and management of the circus, often two hundred strong at these moments, looked over and wondered which performer had earned that gigantic cheer. Then the performers would quickly look back at the arena floor to see who among them had caused that reaction. By then, I was long gone and the conspiracy was our little secret. It thrilled me to make that human connection, and in a mischievous way, cause the sensation among twenty thousand audience members, and cast and crew, that they had missed something really big. I still smile thinking about that.

Probably my favorite thing to do in the big arenas was to walk slowly up the long set of stairs, as Grandma of course, then casually walk through a row of seats to the very long banister at the end of the seating section. Let me amend that: a very, very, very long banister. I would slowly climb onto the banister and face headfirst while I slid down as fast as possible. Then I would use my body and my costume to break just before the bottom. I never flew off, but there were times where I could smell burning material from all the friction. In Tucson, Arizona, there was just one section of seats, no balcony, and each side went quite far up. That week, I burned through three coats. Costly, but, what a rush!

On my very first opening night of the Big Apple Circus at Lincoln Center in New York, I (as Grandma) was quietly walking around the reception tent just outside the main big-top right before show time. A Lincoln Center security officer walked up to me and asked to see my ticket. I thought this might be fun, so I reached into my carpetbag and pulled out a Liberace concert ticket from three years before and showed him, not saying a word. He looked at it and said, "Uh oh." He called over a New York City policeman; with one of them on each arm, they escorted me out of the tent. I was in full clown makeup…at the circus. They must have thought I was a crazy person, but, I let them think that. The overture started for the show – opening night, my first show ever at Lincoln Center – and I started to panic, since I was stuck outside. Just then, an acrobat from the show arrived and I asked for his help. He identified me as being a part of the show and they released me so I could run like hell backstage to get ready for my first entrance.

Whew…

I was inducted into the Sarasota Ring of Fame in 2012, the highest honor in American Circus. The following is the transcript from my Ring Of Fame Induction Speech.

January 15, 2012

Thank you all for being a part of this great day in my life and in my career. Thank you to my sponsors; Big Apple Circus; The Altoona Circus Fans of America Tent named after Grandma; to my daughters, Danielle and Emily Lubin, who have contributed so much to my career and to my happiness, and who continue to make me proud every day; to Paul and Diane Gutheil, who unfortunately couldn't be here today; and to my lovely girlfriend, Ann Hageus, who traveled all the way from Stockholm, Sweden, to be with us today.

And thank you to my parents, who had a wonderful sense of humor and started dressing me like a girl at the age of two.

Thank you to all the members of the Ring of Fame for choosing to present me with the greatest honor of my life. I cannot possibly express in words what this means to me. And a special thank you to Floyd Kruger for your great kindness and help.

Congratulations to my fellow inductees for all that you have contributed to the circus; it is a great honor to be amongst you here today.

Laughing so hard, sitting next to Karen DeSanto, I used a zillion Kleenexes at my roast at the 40th Reunion of Clown College, Baraboo, Wisconsin 2008. Photo by Greg DeSanto

There aren't a lot of awards for us clowns. I was lucky enough that David Orr campaigned to add my name to the Altoona Circus Fans tent. I am a 2002 inductee into the International Clown Hall of Fame, though my induction was put in question because, like Pete Rose, I was found to have bet on "circus," but they let me in, anyway. I am a Sarasota Circus Celebrity; my costume is in the Tibbals Learning Center at the John and Mable Ringling Museum of Art. I received the Lou Jacobs Lifetime Achievement Award from Clown Alley.net, and I was just named a Legend of the Macy's Thanksgiving Day Parade, but this is, by far, the most fantastic of all. This is American Circus. The real award, the true honor, is

Michael Bongar, Jeff Gordon, and moi! Clown College Reunion Sarasota, Florida 2013. Photo by Hogan Martley Sedrin

to have been a part of the American Circus for all these years.

Thank you to my friends who are here today, including my dearest childhood friend, Mike Seiden, who taught me my first circus trick over fifty years ago: spinning a pillow on my finger.

Thank you to the fans without whom this event would not be possible, and to my biggest fan, David Orr, for championing me in so many ways over the years. Without the fans, this industry wouldn't be possible, as we all know. When I was a First-of-May with Ringling in 1975, I was actually told to stay away from the circus fans, because they were weird. I am here to say…you are.

Thank you to all the producers and directors and owners who have kept me and my family fed for thirty-seven years: Irvin and Kenneth Feld, Tommy and Struppi Hanneford, Ian Garden, Jr., Mike Naughton, John and Mary Ruth Herriot, Dolly Jacobs, Pedro Reis, and so many more. Thank you to Paul Binder, who dreamed of creating a circus for New York, and then saw me crashing a skateboard into a hockey wall at Madison Square Garden and gave me a home for twenty-five years. I am forever grateful to you.

Thank you to Clown College for birthing me into this world. I am honored to be the first Clown College graduate inducted and I am sure there will be many others. Thank you Kenneth and Irvin Feld, for dreaming up this incredible institution and for hiring me for five seasons on "The Greatest Show on Earth," giving me my introduction into this fantastic world. Thank you especially to Kenneth Feld for looking like me.

My career was born in 1974 at Clown College at the Venice Arena. According to Mapquest, that is 22.6 miles from this very spot. Thirty-seven years, 22.6 miles. That means my career has gone .61 miles per year. That really sucks!

Thank you to the great clowns in history who have preceded me into the Ring of Fame, from Lou Jacobs, to Emmett Kelly, to Felix Adler, to Bello Nock, and many more. Their legacy and their contributions to this art form will live forever; they truly paved the way for all the clowns who followed, including me. In July of 2001, Time Magazine called Bello Nock "America's Best Clown." In response to that, I have spent the past eleven years trying to grow my hair. It is obviously hopeless.

I am lucky enough to have worked with both Bello and Lou. Lou was my teacher in Clown College and my mentor when we worked together on the Red Unit of Ringling. He never hesitated to offer advice when asked; Lou is one of my all-time heroes. I can share one of Lou's secrets to his great success: Lou loved people so much that he devoted seven decades of his life to entertaining them. And the audiences loved Lou back tenfold. He never once mentioned loving the audience when we talked about clowning. But I knew, and millions of people all over America knew in their hearts, that he truly did love them. As I peeked into the arena and watched him bring down the house night after night on Ringling, I aspired to be one-tenth the clown that Lou Jacobs was. Right now, I am one-fifteenth, so I am getting there.

With Shelby Roper, one of my favs on the ship! Photo by LaVahn Hoh

And I am lucky enough to have worked with quite a few others so honored here at the Ring of Fame: Gunther Gebel Williams, who taught me what hard work and humility and devotion truly means; Tommy Hanneford, who taught me what being a true showman is all about; Dolly Jacobs, who taught me that true beauty had nothing to do with how beautiful you look on the outside, but it sure doesn't hurt; Pedro Reis, who taught me that giving up isn't an option, no matter how often people tell you that you will fail. And now, because of him, Circus City U.S.A has its own jewel box of a circus: Circus Sarasota.

Grandma was born here in Sarasota. When I was at Clown

Snorkeling in Dominica, WHALE! Photo by Liv Chanter

College, I was told not to be a Salvation Army clown – to invest my time and energy into designing and building my own costume. So I immediately went to the Salvation Army store in Sarasota and bought what was the prototype of Grandma during my first winter quarters. Grandma's first appearance was in Venice on January 1, 1975. Though I didn't get a single laugh that day, I did get a lot of attention. The effect was as if someone had accidentally wandered out of the audience onto the hippodrome track of the circus. In fact, most of the audience looked like Grandma. That attention was the first encouragement I received in my professional career, and I felt instantly that this character was something I needed to develop. I must have done something right.

In 1982, I made my debut with the Big Apple Circus at Lincoln Center in New York City. Before the show, I was walking around the reception tent in character and a Lincoln Center security guard asked me for a ticket. I reached into my carpetbag and pulled out a ticket to a Liberace concert from three years before. He muttered, "Uh oh," called over a New York City policeman, and with one on each arm, they threw me out. I was wearing full clown makeup and my Grandma garb at a CIRCUS, and they threw me out. I must have done something right.

Years later while appearing on my skateboard during the Great Milwaukee Circus Parade, I was thrown out of the Parade by Milwaukee's finest. Here I was in a CIRCUS parade, in full clown regalia, and they threw me out. In fact, they nearly arrested me. I must have done something right.

Years later, here I am, in full male regalia, in front of so many fans and circus folks; family and friends; Swedes and New Jerseyites; being inducted into the Ring of Fame. (Look around, waiting for someone to throw me out.) Isn't anyone gonna throw me out? I know that to be standing here before you today, in the Mecca of American circus – to Sarasota, Florida – to be so honored by the Ring of Fame for my thirty-seven-year career, I must have done something right. And I'm not done yet. Thank you.

> A quick wink from a stranger across a subway platform can mean only one thing. Cat hair.

Semester at Sea – Fall 2012

When I knew that my contract with Big Apple Circus was due to expire, I felt that the perfect segue into the next phase of my life would be to teach a full semester with the floating university, "Semester at Sea." I had done partial voyages before and loved the sea, the people, the travel, and the ports. I applied for and was accepted as a full-time professor. Dreams do come true.

On August 18, 2012, I boarded the M.V. Explorer, a former cruise ship turned floating college campus, and didn't disembark until December 7. During that time, I hung out with an astronaut; had the U.S. Ambassador to Brazil ask if he could join me for breakfast (twice); performed at a church for poor schoolchildren in Ghana; visited an even poorer orphanage and then Nelson Mandela's cell at Robben Island in South Africa; hung out on the beaches of England, Portugal, Spain, Uruguay, and Brazil; and snorkeled in Dominica. I listened to an alarming speech about world security issues by the former head of the CIA; sailed up the Amazon into the very heart of the South American continent to the steamiest and most remote place I have ever been; saw people smiling broadly as they were living in the worst poverty I have ever experienced; tangoed in Argentina; taught a workshop to people dedicating their lives to clowning for children in hospitals in Belgium; and mourned the loss of a student who died tragically during our semester. Pure ecstasy and pure agony.

The University of Virginia administers the semester abroad program, which is quite unique. Instead of students taking a semester overseas in one location, this program invites English-speaking students worldwide to embark on a voyage in which they travel to many countries, study while at sea, then enjoy the culture, geography, arts, and people while in port. I was hired as Artist in Residence to teach "The Unique Genre of Physical Comedy" as part of the thirty-two-member faculty. Anyone who has ever been lucky enough to sail with Semester at Sea will tell you that it is a life-changing experience.

Semester at Sea, Fall 2012, try and find me, I am there on the MV Explorer

All the ports were amazing, though my favorite times were when we were all on board, traveling across short and long expanses of water; socializing and sharing stories; teaching, learning together, laughing. The times at sea were among the most inspiring and peaceful moments of my life, and getting to know people young and old under those conditions was a thrill I will never forget. I crave taking another voyage.

I learned to lower my expectations in each port, because it was simply impossible to do all the things I wanted in a place I might never visit again. I decided to do one cool thing each day in each port. If I accomplished that, I didn't stress, even if I saw nothing else. A day on the beach at Ipanema in Rio de Janiero; performing two shows with my girlfriend, Ann, in Ghana; discovering the majestic beauty of South Africa; a tango show and lesson in Argentina. It was more than enough, and yet, it will never be enough for this adrenaline junkie.

My class on board consisted of twenty very different in-

My class at Semester at Sea, maybe my lecture about the wonders of lead pencils wasn't their thing. Photo by Barry Lubin

dividuals who had twenty very different reasons for taking my physical comedy class. At the beginning of the semester, I asked how many of them were planning to pursue show business careers. Four raised their hand. As we neared the end of the voyage, I asked the same question. Three raised their hand. I still can't decide whether that meant that I had a positive or negative influence on the fourth student.

On days when the ship was rocking and rolling at sea, we marched out to the back deck to escape the queasiness, but I kept on teaching as best I could. We laughed a lot and learned so much from each other. To keep things interesting, we would do a bit of what I call "guerilla clowning." We escaped the classroom and disrupted something or someone on the ship for just a brief moment and then quickly returned to the classroom. I made sure we never did something we would later regret, nor totally wreak havoc on anyone or anything. One day on the back deck, we were practicing a group clown slapping exercise where I would act as if I were slapping the entire troupe. I noticed, inside the dining area behind us, that two students were watching us instead of studying. I turned around and slapped them, and they took the slap perfectly. A great moment for all of us.

At times, we would just drag whoever was walking by into our classroom and have them join us in a random exercise. Other times, I would throw one of the students out. It was all designed to keep them happy, focused, intrigued, on their toes, and involved. One of the hardest things to deal with in the unique atmosphere that is Semester at Sea was getting the student's attention the morning after they came back from three days of partying on the beach in Rio, or are about to disembark in the next port to go cave exploring, or hang gliding, or flying off to Greece. Their attention was hard to get and keep at times, unless we were in the middle of a twelve-day crossing of the Atlantic Ocean. Talk about captive

My Physical Comedy class aboard the MV Explorer, Semester at Sea Fall 2012. Photo by Niles Grat

audiences.

One time we left the classroom and quietly marched into Academic Dean LaVahn Hoh's office and sang "Happy Birthday" to him, even though we knew full well it wasn't his birthday. There were twenty-one of us crammed in the tiny office with LaVahn. We marched out immediately after the song. A few days later, LaVahn walked into my physical comedy class unannounced, stood in the front, and gave everyone a clown slap, which is not a real slap at all. With a classic deadpan expression on his face, he took his hand and swiped it far from anyone's face from left to right. My entire class clapped their hands together and took his "slap" as they reacted by moving their faces from left to right. He then left the classroom as randomly as he had arrived, leaving us all laughing our asses off.

Their final was a physical comedy performance, which they wrote themselves, for the entertainment of the entire shipboard community in the theater/lecture hall. In fact, they wrote the entire show the day before and the day of the final performance. My class all passed with flying colors, and it was a night to remember for us all. To be paid to make people laugh is wonderful. To teach others to make people laugh is exquisite. And my class, well, they were funny as hell. I loved my class and still communicate with a few who took the course.

LaVahn Hoh and his wife, M.F., are dear friends, and are the reason I got the gig. LaVahn was in charge of hiring the faculty. Without the support of LaVahn, there is probably no way the University of Virginia would have been confident enough to hire me for a semester as Artist in Residence. I may be the only college dropout in the fifty-year history of Semester at Sea to have ever taught an accredited course on board the ship. Lavahn is simply one of the greatest friends a person could have and I owe him and M.F. a lot. I believe it is up to around $18.74. He got me on board in 2008 for a week as a guest lecturer, and for three weeks in 2010 when he served as Academic Dean for the first time. The summer of 2010 was the first time I had ever crossed the ocean on a ship and it scared the crap out of me, but I survived.

I have him to thank for that experience.

There was a surreal feeling to the sheer number of incredible experiences we were all piling up in our lives during the fall 2012 voyage. We sailed up the Amazon and observed a tremendous amount of the rain forest being burned. We were appalled. I had numerous meals with Kathy Thornton, a former NASA astronaut, who graciously allowed me to ask lots of ridiculous questions about space travel, and patiently answered them all. That alone was one of the biggest thrills of my life. I body surfed on the southwest coast of Spain. Exquisite! I toured the caves inside the Rock of Gibraltar. The World War Two history lesson left me speechless, as did the resident monkeys. I woke up and looked out of my cabin to see hundreds of sea birds in the middle of the ocean following the ship and was reminded that the world is an amazing and mysterious place. I crossed longitude and latitude zero, the intersection of the prime meridian and the equator, and observed how this simple thing – a rarity in nautical travel – made every person on board excited and happy all at once, including me! I watched wild zebras grazing on a hillside within the city limits of Cape Town, South Africa. I smelled things in Ghana that I thought would never leave my nostrils while riding through a poverty-stricken fishing village, and when I told my girlfriend, Ann, I could never live that way, she replied that I could and would if the choice was that or death. I took a subway ride to the wrong end of the line and ended up walking six hours through the streets of Buenos Aires, enabling me to see the city in a way I never could have planned or intended. It was exhausting and exhilarating. I went to the beach in Montevideo, Uruguay, by day, and watched the U.S. election results broadcast live in my hotel room at night. I had my friend, M.F., take a photo of me with two women in thongs on the beach at Ipanema, though they thought I wanted them to take a photo of us. The whales, the dolphins, the albatross following the ship for days; the seals, the flying fish; the waves, the sunsets, the people: these fleeting moments are etched forever in my memory, and there were so many more from this voyage.

I had never witnessed beauty like I did in South Africa. The majesty of the sea meeting the mountains, the surreal vistas, the beautiful penguin colonies, and wild zebras and baboons. When we arrived in port, just before the ship was cleared and all could disembark in Cape Town, the U.S. Consulate representatives told us horror stories about traveling into the city and into the townships. The man in charge of the security of U.S. citizens told us that if we walk up to an ATM and there are wires attached to it, hit the ground because it is about to blow up. Semester at Sea officials said, before our arrival into Cape Town, that seeing the real South Africa required going into the townships, but the head of security for U.S. citizens visiting Cape Town told us he would never go there. There had been too many random and violent encounters, and he strongly suggested we choose something else to do. The ship had already booked quite a few such trips, so it gave us all pause, to say the least. I am a very conservative person and was really nervous about doing that.

After several days visiting various parts of the area around Cape Town, we decided to take someone's advice and go to a fantastic restaurant, which happened to be located in a township and was visited every day by the upper crust of Cape Town and township residents alike. The food at Mzoli's Meat was that good.

We took a taxi and the scene was chaotic, though at the same time reassuring. We met some friends who had hired a tour guide and ate a fantastic meal with them. At this restaurant, you chose your meat at the counter; they cooked it up and you ate it inside a tented structure pulsating with loud music and life. One couldn't help bobbing to the loud music, and we ate the meat using our hands, because the only other option was a plastic spoon on a paper plate.

My girlfriend, Ann, looked over at me, knowing how conservative I was, and asked, "Hating it?" I told her no – I was actually loving it. After that, we joined our friends and entered another township where the tour guide introduced us to a family living in relatively middle-class style. I learned that, in the townships, there was a distinct lower, middle, and upper class. The woman who owned this house was very nice; she showed us her home, which was a combination of appalling and normal. She had electricity, a stove, and television, but she also had a toilet outside that didn't work and a crowd of disintegrating huts behind the house where her kids lived. Her sister, whom she explained had AIDS and was drunk most of the time, came over to visit and insisted we visit her house, which we avoided as politely as possible. She was so spectacularly drunk that the idea seemed quite unappealing at the time.

Then our friends said they wanted to play soccer with some locals in the township, just to do it. We went in search of a soccer ball and rounded up a few people and just started to kick the ball around, until a few kids joined us. I sat it out because I am not much of a soccer player, but at the end of the game, we were all just having a ball together, and we realized that this international sport simply brought the world together – young and old, well-off and poverty-stricken. I made the kids laugh, bridging more gaps, and they made me laugh in return. It was fun, and that was all it needed to be. As we left the township, our guide told us in an emotional way that we had made a real difference in their lives that day. I asked him how. He explained that the people we met, to whom we'd revealed ourselves and vice-versa, received a great lesson in how people had so much in common, even if their preconceptions were that we were not like them. That was ironic to me, because I felt exactly the same.

In Ghana, the smiles of the schoolchildren were so beautiful, and yet they had nothing to play with in their schoolyard except for one dusty old tire. One. I felt terrible for them, but they didn't feel that way about themselves. It is the way life is for them in Tema. As we traveled to new ports and experienced new places, people, and cultures, we were all encouraged to look at the similarities and not the differences. In retrospect, I realized that if we look at the person beneath the trappings of poverty or wealth anywhere on earth, we are all so similar. It is comforting to know that, for some reason.

My girlfriend and I did two performances there and the first went pretty badly. We got into costume in front of them, and though I had the full Grandma look with us, I only partially wore her ensemble (no wig) because of the equatorial heat. My initial response to this failure was that I had no idea about how to judge the sense of humor of the entire African continent. We did a second show at a nearby school/orphanage and they had a great time with us, their laughter being the kind that any clown would want to hear anywhere on earth. It was simply a great experience and honor to work for these kids in both shows.

A moment I will never forget occurred as we left Rio. As we boarded the ship, the famous Christ the Redeemer Statue, which overlooks the city, was fully shrouded in fog. Just as we left the port, the fog parted; as we sailed away from Rio, the statue, now visible, was surrounded in a light fog for thirty miles. It was like the statue was seeing to it that our journey was secure.

I snorkeled our first day in the last port, Dominica, and when I returned to the ship with a few students, we learned that one of our students had died in a boating accident. The emotions on board ship were indescribable.

A beautiful life cut short.

We sailed away from Dominica the next evening without her. It was a totally helpless feeling and too awful for words. The waters were calm that night and the ship sailed smoothly under the light of the moon. Almost all the decks were clear of people. All you could hear was the slice of the water under the ship and muffled sobs from behind cabin doors.

When we disembarked in Ft. Lauderdale a few days later, we all went our separate ways. After living, eating, breathing, celebrating, and mourning together for one hundred and seven days, we were no longer connected physically. But we will always be connected spiritually. As my flight lifted off the runway, I tried to catch a glimpse of the ship…and then I began to sob uncontrollably.

> Don't ever be afraid to tell someone they are smelly unless that person is too.

I Fell in Love All Over Again

I am in love with a wonderful woman who happens to be from Sweden. Ann Hageus and I first met in 1986, though I don't remember it. (Too stoned.) What I do remember is 1990, when Ann was hired as the Big Apple Circus chiropractor/physical therapist/masseuse. I fell in love with her in 1990, but nothing happened. She was not in love, and I was married with a daughter, and with another daughter soon to be born. While nothing happened, our paths had crossed and a seed was planted. Ann went back to Europe after four months of working with the circus. She got married, had three children, and led a good life.

On December 26, 2004 – on the last day of their family vacation on an idyllic beach in Thailand – her family was destroyed by a wave. Her son, Gosta, was taken by the tsunami that claimed over two hundred thousand souls. Their lives were never to be the same.

In August 2008, eighteen years after I had last seen her, Ann contacted me, wondering if I would mind a visitor for the holidays in December. I was days away from cancer surgery, and her call brightened my life when I needed it the most. She arrived on December 29 and it was the beginning of a love story – and, unexpectedly, a big career change for us both. Ann was a chiropractor and I was under a long contract with Big Apple Circus.

Three weeks after Ann returned to Sweden, I found out that she and her daughter, Karin, would be attending a circus performance. I wanted to surprise her by showing up at the Cirkus Cirkor show in a theater in Stockholm called Dansens Hus, but there were no tickets to be had. I told my friend, Mark Gindick, about my plight, and he said simply, "Why not just ask to be in the show?"

Impossible! I thought.

But I emailed the artistic director, Tilde Bjorfors, anyway. Amazingly, she said they'd love to have me.

I arrived painfully early in the morning to Stockholm and checked into a hotel near the theater. I slept for eight hours and then went to a rehearsal with FeFe, the resident clown of Cirkus Cirkor at the time. He decided that I would appear at the end of the intermission, where I would seem to be a little old lady who wandered accidentally onto the stage. I got into makeup and costume early and watched the entire first half from the wings, where I enjoyed a great performance. I peeked into the audience once during the first half to see if I could find Ann and Karin, but I could not. I didn't want to chance ruining the surprise, so I remained very discreet.

Intermission was nearly over and FeFe said it was time. I walked out into the audience and wandered up onto the stage. The seats where I knew Karin and Ann would be sitting were empty. I did a few bits on stage, and the audience responded very nicely for my first time performing in Sweden. Then, I saw Ann and Karin, and my heart leaped. They were waving at me as they returned to their seats from intermission. I finished my bit, and Fefe and his partner, as we had rehearsed earlier, insisted I get off the stage so the show could resume. There wasn't an empty seat in the eight-hundred-seat theater except one: next to Ann. (The man who had been sitting there during the first half of the circus hadn't returned.)

I walked off the stage into the audience and plopped myself down next to my sweetie. Eight-year-old Karin looked at me very strangely, and Ann looked at me even more oddly as the second half began. (I love surprises, as long as they aren't happening to me.) Karin asked her mom, after my first visit to Sweden, if we had a "chance" with each other – a Swedish expression.

Chances were...good. Because five years later, Ann and I appeared together as a clown team on that very same stage.

Ann joined me on a gig in New Zealand a few years ago at the World Buskers Festival. It was the first time in thirty years that I had to pass the hat to make money. I wondered what the universe was telling me when I took that gig. The problem was I actually felt guilty passing the hat at the end of my shows. Substance is important, but not always as important as the pitch at the end. I would watch some performers harangue the audience for ten minutes explaining, imploring, and bullying them into opening their wallets. It was really anti-show biz, but this wasn't show biz. It was a form of begging, but with a stage and a sound technician, and hotel and airfare provided. I did quite poorly. My performances went over well, but out of guilt and my sense of show, I simply asked them to be generous and "thank you very much." I got lots of laughs, but very little cash.

After a few days visiting her with her son, Julius, who was studying for a year in Australia, Ann joined me for the last three days of the festival, where I talked her into helping me out. It was the first time we had ever "worked" together and she was very reluctant and nervous. At the end of the show, I explained, "I am actually a guy and this is my Swedish girlfriend, Ann, and she will now explain how it works." Ann spoke in Swedish for about forty-five seconds, with the audience and me looking at her dumfounded. Then I took the microphone and said, "I have no idea what she said, but she's adorable and cooks really well. Ann will be out there in the crowd and I will stay by the stage, so please give generously."

The "hat" doubled. I have been lucky enough to be paid to do shows for decades, but there was something cool about taking that cash and turning it into meals and car rentals and hotel rooms, which we did right after the gig ended, touring incredible New Zealand. That is where Ann got the performing bug again after so many years.

When Ann was young, she went to a professional circus school for a year in Paris – Ecole au Carre – and fell in love with that world, but left to do something more sensible with her life. She became a chiropractor, married a great guy, and had three great kids. But the circus found a way to call her back, and I was to provide her doorway into that world once again.

She was my "audience volunteer" for a water-spitting act at a festival called Kleines Fest in Hannover, Germany, in 2010. The audiences loved her. The act consisted of me spitting water in various ways, and then teaching an audience member how to do it. For three shows a day, for three weeks, they loved her. The reactions for the act were perhaps the biggest of my career, and it shocked me. I would never have chosen a woman as my volunteer for the water-spitting act because it never felt politically correct to literally spit water on a woman, but the reactions were spectacular. The fact that I play a female character, and also the fact that the audience volunteer got me plenty wet probably made a difference. Ann was hooked, and we have enjoyed performing together in circuses, schools, theaters, and festivals in the U.S., Africa, and Europe ever since.

Ann and I have always talked about our hopes and dreams, and once I revealed my desire to bring a show to Broadway. She asked, "Well, what is stopping you?" That simple question led to a major life and career change, and in July of 2012, my deal with the Big Apple Circus expired and the world became my oyster in a new way. I moved to Sweden and began freelancing as a clown, director, writer, mentor, and teacher. And I soon hope to bring my Broadway dream to life. It is a bit scary, and I know I might not realize this important wish on top of my bucket list, but to not try isn't an option. Sweden is beautiful, and an enormous change for me. It isn't New York, so I travel to New York as much as possible, especially to see my kids. Oh, and the bagels and caffeine-free Diet Coke. Plenty of tuna in Stockholm.

There is nothing Ann would rather do than buy a caravan and travel and perform with a circus. I love the circus and perform shorter engagements quite often. Unfortunately, I am at the stage in my life where I have been there and done that. I am happy that I did all that touring, but I am ready for other challenges. Just the thought of touring again like that exhausts me, but if someone offered us a tour of New Zealand or Australia or another exotic part of the world that I would love to visit, I would consider it just for Ann. Readers, book us! My usual financial terms are...

Ann's journey from the total devastation caused by the tusnami in 2004 to her new career as a clown is amazing in many ways. Instead of giving up on life by letting the pain and depression overtake her, she chose to bring light, laughter, and love to others. She is simply a beautiful and wonderful person, whom I love very dearly.

In 2009, Ann wrote a book called To Live on Anyway, which was released in Sweden, and in February of 2014, that same book was translated to English and re-released in the U.S. and worldwide by, coincidentally, my publisher. The book was her way of grieving and dealing with the loss of her son. I couldn't be prouder of her efforts to not only heal, but to share that pain with the world to help others who are dealing with the same.

> **Some enchanted evening, you may wear an adult diaper.**

The Clown Walks Away

My Ring of Fame plaque unveiled 2012, from left, Kenneth Feld, Ann Hageus, Emily Lubin, Danielle Lubin, Chuck Sidlow, back row, Armando Gaona, Bill Troxell, David Orr, Joel Dein, Paul Binder. Photo by Dr. Zachary Fantrim

There is an imperceptible line, a microscopic border that separates the audience from the ring in any circus. When I was in treatment for cancer, that line became very thick. I longed to cross the barrier and into the delicious sawdust, but I could not. Life put that on hold as I took care of my health. I ached for it. I had a gift for the audience, but I couldn't give it. When I was healthy enough to pass through the invisible thin line and back into the ring again, my elation was impossible to describe. It was like a child getting to go back into his or her favorite playground after it being closed for a few weeks. I stepped back into the ring of the Big Apple Circus on opening night in New York in October of 2008 like a happy little kid, and the playground was mine once again.

It was in Brooklyn, in May of 1982, where my love affair began with the audiences of the Big Apple Circus. Over the course of twenty-five seasons and thousands of performances, I simply tried to make people laugh. In that beautiful ring, I cried, danced, lifted off the ground for just a few moments carrying a small child in my arms, tumbled, spit water, rode a horse, played drums, joked with celebrities, performed on a trapeze, and countless other things. I shared the

My plaque at the Ring of Fame, and Linda Zeswitz who had just cleaned bird poop off of it. Photo by Andrew Zeswitz

Ring of Fame with Big Apple Circus Founder Paul Binder. Photo by Emily Lubin

ring with the greatest circus artists and the loveliest audience members in the world. I was a tiny part of people's lives, and I was touched by their love. I learned a great deal about myself and the world, and in the process, I had the time of my life.

On May 13, 2012, in Boston, I crossed the invisible line surrounding the ring for the final time. The men who had hired me, Paul Binder and Michael Christensen, congratulated me. The audience stood in my honor and I sobbed. A few hours later, I was on an airplane headed to Germany for my next engagement. That is show business in a nutshell. One moment, a celebration and standing ovation and tears. The next, sitting alone at Logan Airport, waiting to fly off to Europe. My clowning career was far from over, but my quarter-century with the Big Apple Circus was, and with it, many chapters of my life came to a close.

I don't know what the future holds for me, but I welcome it with open arms. Long after I'm gone, Grandma will live on. Because of this simple little character, I was able to contribute something to the world, even if it was just laughs.

They say that when you are on your deathbed, you won't wish that you'd spent more time at the office. In my case, they couldn't be more wrong.

People Who Made A Difference

There are many people who have touched my life and made me who I am today. They molded and shaped me in many ways. Some were only there for parts of my existence, others throughout. Sharing my story without telling you how they helped my life and career wouldn't be fair to them, and would only paint a partial picture of who I really am. The hard part about recognizing people who are so important to your life is that their effects on you are not always obvious or clear. Most of the time, it's not until years later that you realize how they influenced you. In order to be truthful to them and to myself, I've decided to dedicate this part of my book to the "village who raised a transvestite" by introducing many of them to you, one by one. It would be impossible to include everyone who truly belongs on this list, but here goes...

My Mom
Unconditional love. Edythe Lubin loved to laugh, and in her younger days was a real beauty – glamorous and popular. It is amazing how having a family can screw that up, but it never screwed up her sense of humor. I loved to make her laugh. She never understood why I used to go to bed with my window open in the dead of winter. I refused to get out of bed in the morning, and she would curse like crazy as she came in, close the window, and sometimes even stop to scrape up the snow that was accumulating just below the windowsill. I guess I was spoiled. Mom was the foundation upon which I built my life.

Danielle and Emily Lubin
The warmest feeling in the world to me is seeing my children grow up to become incredibly beautiful individuals. They have my unconditional love as no one else does on this earth, and their warmth and good hearts have been a great example for me, and for the people in their lives whom they touch. Danielle and Emily are the coolest people I know. Poor them – having not only having a father who is a clown, but one who wears dresses. They are my foundation now.

Ann Hageus
My love and my hero in countless ways. Her ability to live on having lost her middle child, and to reinvent herself from a career as a chiropractor to becoming a working performance artist, was a great inspiration to me and to so many others. She is all about values, principals, love. She taught me to be a better person. We share our lives together in Stockholm, Sweden.

Mike Seiden
My earliest childhood friend growing up in Ventnor, New Jersey. He taught me how to spin a pillow on my finger, a skill that, for some reason, wowed my fellow clowns in the circus. This beautiful man and his beautiful wife, Amy, stuck by me through thick and thin for well over fifty years with fierce loyalty. Rock-solid friends, full of kindness, generosity, love. Words could never describe what Mike and Amy mean to me. In fact, there are quite a few other Seidens who belong on this list along with Mike. They always treated me like family.

Roberta Lubin
As my wife, she supported and helped my career, and raised two amazing and wonderful daughters – often alone, while I was on the road trying to support our family. How much bigger a hero can a person be in one's life than that? Roberta also taught me the value of charity and giving back to society, and I try to accommodate those requests for my time and my resources as often as possible. When Roberta replaced me as Grandma in a Big Apple Circus show with two hours notice when I came down with chicken pox, she walked around in the audience beforehand, as I often did as Grandma, and as people responded to her then, she told me she truly understood for the first time why I needed to continue to play the character. She felt the love.

Evie Kelly Lentz
The widow of American icon clown Emmett Kelly, arguably the most famous American clown in history. Evie generously shared with me some of the most important secrets that made Emmett as great, beloved, and as famous a clown as he became. One of the best things anyone ever said to me was when Evie told me, "You

are my second-favorite clown." Evie floored me when she casually suggested I take Emmett's famous spotlight routine, the most iconic clown routine in memory, which involved sweeping a spotlight with a broom in the most delightful, funny, and charming ways. I told her that everyone would think I stole it from Emmett if I started doing it. Her response: "Screw 'em."

Judy Weisman
Judy went from being a dancer at Radio City Music Hall to becoming a surgeon. Judy migrated from her hometown of New York City to the great north country of upstate New York to raise a family and run a very successful medical practice. We met on a ski slope in Vermont with her kids, Gabe and Dana, and we hit it off right away. Judy has always been there for me, even when I have been a true pain in the ass asking her for medical advice at all hours of the day and night from all over the world. Judy likened her operating room to a theatrical stage, where she played the lead actor, director, and stage manager, as she had to command the room. Judy is the definition of a "rock." She's not only my rock, but one for many others.

D.F. Sweedler
An eccentric man, a cerebral man, a beautiful man. D.F. started his career as a comedian in New York comedy clubs the same year I became a clown. He was my college roommate at Emerson College for three years; he never let me down for any reason, held me up when I was down, listened to me, and still does so after over four decades of friendship. He was a brilliant teacher and writer of comedy, and made me laugh A LOT! I have tried many times over the years to push D.F. into bushes for absolutely no reason, but was never successful. With some hidden superhuman strength, he resisted, but never tried to push me into a bush even once. A true gentleman, a beautiful friend.

Michael Bongar
Michael produced events and booked talent in places around the globe. Michael is the person who I always counted on for excellent business and personal advice. But much more than that, Michael was a gentle soul who a great many people have counted on for help, in good weather or bad. Michael was the very definition of

the Yiddish word "mensch." Because Michael was very dry and superbly iconic, he was easily the most imitated producer on the New York scene by those performers who loved and respected him and who were lucky enough to work with him. In the shark-infested world of New York show business, Michael and his partner/wife, Tina, were the sweetest, most genuine people I could possibly know. They brilliantly booked me four times on The Late Show with David Letterman at the Ed Sullivan Theater in New York, one of my all-time greatest thrills. Michael also booked me at a mall in Paramus.

LaVahn and M.F. Hoh

LaVahn was a professor in the Theater Department at the University of Virginia, and his wife, M.F., worked there for decades keeping the department running smoothly. I am ridiculously lucky to have them in my life. They have employed me, fed me, housed me, and been lovely friends. LaVahn and M.F. have been unreasonably kind to me ever since I first met them. My test of new comedy material is whether it makes LaVahn turn red from laughter, which is both a great compliment and quite concerning.

Joel Dein

Joel was the Director of Communications at Big Apple Circus and enjoyed a few previous careers, including folk singing, and handling Broadway shows and managing Broadway stars. He dedicated himself to helping my career, my image, and most importantly, my life. He was one of those fabulous people who I could always count on through thick and thin. Joel knew how to listen to me bitch and moan, and when I was done, ignore it all. He and his lovely wife, Sandy, are the epitome of warmth. Joel is the executive producer of my first film, The Lady Under the Bleachers, for a very good reason: he has great show business savvy, plus he is incredibly gifted at calming me down when necessary.

Mitch Freddes

A great clown from my Clown College class and early Ringling Circus days, Mitch was a spiritual man who has been a major inspiration to me by re-inventing himself again and again as life threw him curveballs. He has always been like a brother to me. He and I learned how to scream curse words at the top of our lungs from one end of the Ringling arena to the other without ever being busted.

Matt Pauli
Matthew was a great clown in his own right, with a timelessness to his character and his performances. This man, who played Grandma for six tours of Big Apple Circus, dropped everything else in his life when I was sick and unable to perform in 2008. He stepped into the circus earlier and with less rehearsal time than he had ever done before, and allowed me to be away from the circus while I dealt with my illness without any worry.

My brother, Jay Lubin
I love him like a brother, because he is my brother. A man who served our country, his family, and his community with intelligence and a quiet dignity, and who made my life impossible when I was young, because everyone expected me to be just as great as him.

Bob Davies
When Atlantic City High School acquired television production equipment and a fully-loaded studio just before my sophomore year, a few of us were lucky enough to be given keys to the kingdom by Bob Davies, head of the audio/visual committee at the school. We all had to figure out what to do with it. We learned how to make television from scratch. Lubin, Bobby Solomon, Bruce Peskoe, Rob Huberman, and Dean Scarpa combined to become our own little production company, "Lubsolkomanpa." For three years, we wrote, directed, starred, produced, edited, ran sound and cameras for, and created television comedy. Bob taught us that hard work and dedication, along with blind trust by your mentors, can lead to getting past a lot of mistakes on the road to success. Bob was my earliest influence in the direction toward a professional career. Bob Davies trusted and loved us, and we are all better people for it.

Marc Koltnow
Marc is a dear friend who lives in Tucson, Arizona. We became friends in high school when we realized that we shared a very silly sense of humor. He always made me laugh, and I just tried to keep

up with him. He told me about something he had read about called Clown College, and explained that it was a college dedicated just to clowns. We both thought that was the coolest thing. That little conversation struck an unconscious chord inside me, and when I had dropped out after my third year at Emerson College and met a guy who had gone to Clown College the year before, I was instantly reminded of my conversation with Marc. I decided that I had to go for it. I did, and the rest is history. Marc was always far funnier than me, but life takes its turns for whatever reasons, and I went into show business. Marc remains as silly and funny as ever, enjoying the pleasure of being funny without the pressure of having to be.

Bill Ballantine
Before Bill became the Dean of Clown College, he was a very talented artist and circus clown on Ringling. At my audition for Clown College, Bill took a special interest in me for no apparent reason. He personally put me through the paces of the audition, though there were plenty of others auditioning that day at the old Boston Garden in 1974 during Ringling Brothers and Barnum & Bailey's annual engagement. I remember doing a pantomime of a tightrope walk for Bill, and after that, he looked at me with his searing blue eyes for a very long moment. I held his gaze, and something inside me clicked, telling me that I was going to get into Clown College, though nothing was said at the time. Bill made it possible for me to attend, and for years after he never stopped nurturing my development. Bill took me off the traveling unit of Ringling to teach new students in 1976 and 1977, which was a thrill and a real confidence builder for a new clown. I will be forever grateful to Bill for his searing gaze, which luckily landed on me that spring afternoon in New England.

Irvin and Kenneth Feld
The bosses, the producers, the owners, the guys who signed my first professional contracts. Without Irvin and his son, Kenneth, producers of "The Greatest Show on Earth," this book wouldn't be possible. They offered me a contract once I finished Clown College, and they never stopped offering year after year. They generously encouraged me to develop the little old lady right from the day of her debut on January 1, 1975, providing me with numerous

opportunities to do so.

I was offered several contracts over the years, my choice of traveling units of Ringling Brothers and Barnum & Bailey, teaching and consulting work for them, and the best offer I had ever received up to that point: to be the only clown on an all-star circus featuring winners of the International Circus Festival of Monte Carlo, a job I turned down for fear that I just wasn't ready. In 1979, Kenneth took a phone call from me asking to get out of my contract with the Blue Unit of Ringling. He graciously told me to think about it for three weeks, and if I still felt that way, he would grant me my wish. He handled me with respect and class when I opted to leave "The Greatest Show on Earth," and though I still have regrets about walking away that July day in 1979, I won't ever forget how I was treated when I finally asked for my release.

It wasn't much longer after that when Kenneth hired me for some consulting work, and then to teach many more times at Clown College. I often use the lessons I learned from Irvin and Kenneth Feld during those years. Kenneth delivered the most important lesson to me during contract renewal time at the end of my third season on Ringling. I asked for terms that were unacceptable to him, and I was frankly shocked that he said no. Then Kenneth told me, "Barry, we would love to have you under contract, but whether you are here or not next season, there will be twenty-eight clowns on 'The Greatest Show on Earth.'" Though it hurt like hell to learn that my talent and hard work weren't enough to earn a few extra bucks and a bigger space on the circus train, Kenneth delivered the words professionally and without being unkind. The lesson: in show business and in every other business, everyone is expendable. There were twenty-eight clowns that next season on "The Greatest Show on Earth." I was not one of them.

Jimmy Tinsman

Jimmy went to Clown College in 1973, and was a clown on the Ringling show for several years before becoming an integral part of Big Apple Circus. Without my partner from my Ringling days, James Ormsby Tinsman, AKA "Tinseltits," two very significant things would never have happened. I wouldn't have performed at the International Circus Festival of Monte Carlo in 1977, and my twenty-five-year career at Big Apple Circus would never have started in 1982. Jimmy generously put my name forward to Paul

Binder when the need arose for a new act for a corporate circus show outside the Big Top.

Jimmy and I had a great run together, appearing on numerous television shows and at many special events during our Ringling and Big Apple Circus days. We never stopped laughing, counting our good fortune, and enjoying the experiences we were lucky enough to be offered.

Jimmy was invited to join me in 1978 when I was teaching for the first time at Clown College as the full-time Clowning Instructor. I had tried very hard to be as effective a teacher as possible, working to gain the respect of the students of the class of '78. Then Jimmy came off the traveling unit of Ringling; first stop: my class. I had the entire class gathered to introduce them to Jimmy, and to talk about partner clowning, of which he and I had done an awful lot. In the middle of a sentence, Jimmy put his hand on the top of my head, lifted himself high in the air to the point that his butt was in my face, and ripped an enormous fart. I laughed so hard that I fell on the ground in endless fits of laughter. After about five minutes, I was able to stand up and I looked at the students, whose credibility I had worked so hard to gain, and they were just staring incredulously at us. Not a single laugh, giggle, nor smile. The absurdity of the moment led me to explode into another fit of uncontrollable laughter. Jimmy had that effect on a lot of people. He and his wife, Tisha, are the very definition of positivity, and I love them.

Lou Jacobs

The face of Ringling, Lou appeared on posters for "The Greatest Show on Earth" for many years, and I am proud to say, Lou was my friend. Lou was one of the most famous clowns in American circus history, and a U.S. Postal Service® stamp was created in his honor. He mentored many young clowns with a generous spirit. When I worked on the Ringling show with Lou, I watched him perform countless times. I found myself wanting what he had, which was the ability to make people laugh and cry in the same moment with the beauty of his character and his work. His famous words, when asked by young clowns about the art of comedy: "If they laugh, it's funny. If they don't, it's not." Lou entertained more people in his sixty-two years with "The Greatest Show on Earth" than perhaps anyone else. Lou's great secret was simple: he loved the audience and they returned his love a hundredfold over the course of his many years in show business. Lou is an icon whose image is synonymous with clowning worldwide.

Lou was an inspiration to so many generations of clowns. The last quality time I spent with Lou was when he was the guest of honor at The Great Milwaukee Circus Parade and I was performing there in the Royal Hanneford Circus. He was happy to see me and I was thrilled to see him. He was on a tight schedule and many people were trying to get his attention during the weekend of activities. I will never forget when he and I were talking, surrounded by people, and he pulled me aside. Basically, we were just bullshitting with each other and having fun. His handler was getting very impatient and started to interrupt us, telling Lou he had to go. Lou told the man in no uncertain terms, "I will be with you when I am good and ready." I was thrilled that he did that, and we spent some great time together that day. Lou taught me to keep it simple, to work hard, and to give your heart to each audience every show. His daughter, Dolly Jacobs, remains my friend to this day. Along with her husband, Pedro Reis, they created Circus Sarasota, a beautiful one-ring circus in a Big Top tent.

Dick Monday
I met Dick when we were in the same class at the 1974 Ringling Clown College. While living in Hollywood, Richard Milhollan changed his name to Dick Monday. He was one of the most generous partners anyone could hope for, and an incredibly talented man. We performed a silly parody of a Polish juggling act in the final audition show to great response, but we ended up being cast on different units of the traveling Ringling show. Dick lasted a short time on the Blue Unit and then started to make his way in the world of show business in various other venues. We had a chance to work together in 1979 in an Orlando nightclub when nearly no one was doing stand-up comedy. At Disneyland in California in 1986 and 1987, we did three shows a day and learned an enormous amount working together. That led us to create a theater show in Los Angeles where our show, "A Coupla Guys Who Gotta Do a Show," was a Los Angeles Times Pick of the Week.

"A Coupla Guys" was a really fun theater show that combined all the things we learned from our Disney days, along with the character work we developed separately since our Clown College days. Together and in solos we performed a seventy-five-minute show that was fun, inventive, funny, and very much a product of our love for all things silly. Over the years, we have had the chance to philosophize about clowning, and to inspire each other to continue in this noble art. Dick gave me the opportunity to steal any show we were in, and taught me, in turn, how to brilliantly play the straight man. He inspired me with his commitment and creativity. He was always there to support me on stage, no matter what was happening and how we were doing at any given moment. He accomplished all of this with the dignity of a lanky Nebraskan who was just as in love with clowning as I was.

We shared some exquisite moments on stage and in the circus. Perhaps the most important thing Dick taught me was how to teach clowning to others. Every once in a while, we are asked to perform our "Ventriloquist and Dummy" act, a routine originated by me and another partner at Emerson College, recreated with Bill Irwin at Clown College, performed hundreds of times on Ringling and Big Apple Circus with Jimmy Tinsman, and taken to a new level by Dick. We will purposely not talk through or rehearse the routine before performing, even if we haven't run it in years. The memory of this routine is in our bones from our Disneyland days, and regardless of how much time has passed, it never fails to work. Dick is that rare kind of partner who comes along once in a generation, or a lifetime.

Paul Binder
Paul founded the Big Apple Circus, along with his co-founder and partner Michael Christensen, and was its Artistic Director and Ringmaster for many years. Michael rose to fame as "Mr. Stubbs," a modern-day tramp clown. More importantly, Michael founded the Clown Care Program, which inspired people worldwide to create hospital clown groups fashioned after Michael's brilliant vision of providing professional clowns for bedside visits. Paul saw me for the first time in 1978 on Ringling at Madison Square Garden in New York City. I was one of a couple dozen clowns, but he spotted me riding my skateboard into a hockey wall at the Garden and it must have made an impression. When I moved to New York City in 1981, I knocked on his office door on East 104th Street, and thankfully he answered. Like a kid in a candy store, I wanted in. I wanted to be a part of this beautiful, new, one-ring circus founded

by two clowns, which played in the culture center of New York City: Lincoln Center. I told Paul that if the opportunity ever arose to be part of the Big Apple Circus I would love it, and he told me that he remembered the little old lady crashing into a hockey wall. I told him it was unfortunate that the circus had no hockey wall.

The opportunity to audition came just a few months later, and my old partner, Jimmy Tinsman, who was then working at Big Apple Circus, arranged to show Paul a bit that he and I had performed hundreds of times on "The Greatest Show on Earth." Paul was casting for a special engagement the circus was doing outside the Big Top. I will never forget when we went up to his apartment in lower Manhattan, and he was glued to the television watching his beloved New York Giants. When there was a commercial break, he looked over at us for the first time and said, "Okay." Jimmy and I performed the "Ventriloquist and Dummy" act for a few moments in his living room until play resumed, and Paul immediately went back to watching the game.

I figured, Oh well. No chance in hell…

A week later, I was hired.

My first gig for Paul was in Acapulco, Mexico, at the Princess Hotel, a five-star hotel located directly on the ocean. I was hired to do just the ventriloquist act with Jimmy, but I offered to throw in Grandma for free, doing some meet-and-greet with the audience before the show started. He agreed. A few months later, he and Michael Christensen decided to offer me a job with the Big Apple Circus under the Big Top for the spring and summer tour of 1982. I excitedly took the job. And together we built shows for well over two decades featuring Grandma. Paul continues to be one of my biggest supporters.

My fondest memory of Paul was when the city of Chicago gave the Big Apple Circus a hard time regarding our outgoing water supply from the trailers parked at Soldier's Field, and the city wouldn't allow trailers to drain. This went on for several days. Paul and I donned capes and masks one night, and at midnight, we opened the gray water tanks to all the trailers, one by one, causing them to drain. We giggled like schoolboys the entire time. Forgive us, people of Chicago.

Tommy and Struppi Hanneford
Tommy Hanneford was one of the all-time great comedians on

horseback, and Struppi was a world-class aerialist. Together they created the Royal Hanneford Circus many years ago, and earned the reputation of being top-notch producers and for hiring the best talent. Fortunately, for me, they loved my work and they valued comedy, which many producers frankly don't care that much about. When I was unemployed in the late '80s, and worried about how to feed my family, Tommy and Struppi Hanneford were just the medicine I needed. They remedied my situation because they thought I was funny.

Expensive, but funny.

Tommy was one of the greatest showmen in circus history, and it was an honor that he took me under his wing and encouraged me in the simplest way possible: by hiring me. Even though Tommy has long been gone from this earth, Struppi carried on the tradition of great entertainment, and the shows were always a blast in which to perform, especially with one of the great straight men to ever play the role: Ringmaster Billy Martin.

Without the technical budget of Ringling or Big Apple Circus, Tommy and Struppi were only interested in artists who truly connected with the audience with great charisma, and with polish. They hired me for my first solo gig in a three-ring circus in Detroit in the '80s.

Guillaume Dufresnoy

Guillaume was one of the greatest circus aerialists in recent history, and he chose to retire from the air to enjoy safer employment on the ground. Guillaume was my business and artistic manager for the duration of my last contract with Big Apple Circus, a period of nearly thirteen years. During that time, Paul concluded his incredible run as artistic director, and Guillaume was promoted from general manager to become the second artistic director in Big Apple Circus history. He was my manager for quite a few years before he became the artistic director, and his advice kept my profile in the world of international circus in the highest regard possible. He masterfully got me cast in the International Circus Festival of Hungary, a show that launched my career in Europe in 2006.

His aim was to get me to the next level – an invitation to return to the International Circus Festival of Monte Carlo – and his plan worked. I booked that engagement in 2008. We had a great working relationship, which had begun many years before when he was still a performer with Big Apple Circus, but was then in the process of transitioning into a career in management. He was so good at his job that he enabled me to comfortably walk away from the Big Apple Circus at the end of the 2011/2012 season to allow me to pursue other goals in my career in theater, circus, and television, in Europe and around the world.

It was not his intention to see me go, nor to birth the next phase in my career after Big Apple Circus. In fact, he offered me a very generous extension of my contract, which would have taken me five more years to retirement age. I declined. It was simply time to move on for a variety of reasons. Because of Guillaume's decisions, my name became well-regarded nearly everywhere, my performances flourished in Europe as well as at home, and he never stopped challenging me to write the next great clown piece.

At one point near the end of my Big Apple Circus days, Guillaume and I were talking about the process I went through trying to create new material. During the conversation, he said his perception was that I was lazy. I was momentarily floored, but I understood what he meant. I explained that there was nothing I would rather do than create the next great piece of clown material every season, but the agony of the process for me just made it impossible to accomplish every single year. I had perhaps set a standard that was impossible to reach every time I tried. "I am not lazy," I explained, "I wanted to bring back clown pieces I had performed years before, because I couldn't top them in that particular rehearsal time." Because of Guillaume's challenge, I have created a body of original work that may be unparalleled in recent circus clowning history. I am proud of that fact, though I may have lost lots of hair in the process. I may not have succeeded every single year, but perhaps I have added something to the art of clowning, which, to me, is the highest thing I can aspire to.

Merci, Monsieur Dufresnoy.

Merci to all of you…

Barry Lubin

Epilogue

In my dreams, I will make my debut on Broadway, finish the two movie scripts and one play I have started, write a magazine article on female clowns, and create a new show for television along with my talented partner, Yvette Kaplan. I will keep clowning as long as I can, and continue seeing the world on someone else's dime. I will go to Antarctica so I will have visited all of the continents in the world. I will play at Cirque D'Hiver in Paris. I will partner with my love, Ann, and work as a clown duo with her whenever and wherever we can in the world. I will go back to New York as often as possible, not the least reason of which is to see my daughters, Danielle and Emily. I will direct, teach, mentor, write, and bodysurf. I will pass along what I know when the opportunity arises. And I will share Grandma with the world.

I have had ten lifetimes of dreams come true already, and I can't wait to see what the next lifetime brings.

As we say in the circus…

"See you down the road."

And as Grandma would always say:

"Eat your veggies, kids."

Acknowledgments

There are so many people to thank for the successes in my life and in my career. If your name isn't on this list or in this book, please forgive me. Rest assured, I am fairly certain you will be in my next life story.

I approached journalist and author, Heidi Durrow, who wrote the bestseller, The Girl Who Fell From the Sky, and asked if she would interview me as a way of drawing out my story. Heidi considered it for a brief time, but wisely suggested that I write it myself to assure that it was purely my story and my voice. I took Heidi's advice. Thank you, Heidi!

My friend, Claire Rosen, an incredibly creative New York photographer and gown-wearer, sat with me in the Empire Hotel lobby in New York, and had me write down, for thirty minutes, any single word that came to my mind about my life and career. Her reasoning was simple: whatever I wrote would become the keywords from which I would draw my stories, my inspiration, my life tales, my dreams. It was from this list that I began writing Tall Tales of a Short Clown.

Jane and Bob Stine provided priceless feedback, inspiration, and business advice during this journey. I cannot thank Jane enough for looking at my book in its later stages and giving me her honest, professional take on its content. And I cannot thank Bob enough, more famously known as R.L. Stine, for sharing his wisdom and wonderful sense of humor on the subjects of writing, life, and Jane.

I handed over my book to Linda Basilotta Zeswitz for her loving feedback; without realizing it, she edited the book for me. Copious notes, all excellent, leading me toward a much more user-friendly version of my memoirs.

Megan Ivey provided a key influence in the form of supreme encouragement to continue on the path I was heading down, when my writing brain ground to a halt several times.

Ann Hageus, who is a wonderful writer and my life partner, gave me permission to stay up until all hours of the night in our Stockholm home as I agonized over this book, and suffered with my ridiculous sleeping habits that ensued because of it.

My daughters, Danielle and Emily, were always at the forefront of my mind as I wrote about my life; they had an enormous influence on this story. Their love means everything to me. If I am nice enough to them, they might not write their own books revealing the scathing truth about me later on.

Mike Aloisi, my publisher and editor, who not only considered publishing this book well before he had even read it, but who also had the generosity of spirit to publish Ann's beautiful book, To Live On Anyway.

My Ringmasters: the men and women who supported my work as Grandma throughout the years, setting me up for laughs so beautifully, and never taking any of the glory. Tim Holst, Harold Ronk, Kit Haskett, Dinny McGuire, Billy Martin, Paul Binder, Ian Garden, Jr., Senor Ray, Adriana Poema Parker, Mike Naughton, Nikolai Tovarich, Rogier Schol, Charley Hackett, Scott O'Donnell, LaVahn Hoh, Petit Gougou, Alexandr Frish, John Kennedy Kane, Johnny Herriot, Dick Monday, Heidi Herriot, Murat Muturganov, Pedro Reis, Todd Robbins, Becky Kimes, Dan McCallum, Serge Drouard, George Cahill, Dave SaLoutos, Carrie Harvey, Jenna Robinson, Kevin Venardos, and many others.

My clown partners, who had the generosity to let me run wild, and who were always there to pick me up when I fell down, including Jimmy Tinsman, Dick Monday, George Koury, Tiffany Riley, Joel Jeske, Michael Bongar, Rob Torres, Peggy King, Bernice Collins, Judy Beth Ashworth, James Clowney, Carlos Guity, Ted Lawrence, Ray Grins, Erin Grins, Francesco Brunaud,

Guillaume Dufresnoy, Al Calienes, Carlo Pellegrini, Todd Robbins, Mike Naughton, Phil Stein, John Lepiarz, David Casey, Mark Gindick, Michael Christensen, Peter Shub, Scott Nelson, Robb Torres, Muriel Brugman, Jayson Vanderbilt Stewart, Ruth Chaddock, Jeff Gordon, Bello Nock, Rob Slowik, Ann Hageus, and many, many others.

The people who kept my career in the circus and clowning on track when the going got tough, Paul Binder, Tommy and Struppi Hanneford, and Guillaume Dufresnoy.

Those people responsible for helping me reach a level of fame, Joel Dein, Phil Thurston, Barbara Pflughaupt, Liz Ward, and Lizzie Grubman from Big Apple Circus; the many promoters and P.R. people from Ringling Brothers and Barnum & Bailey Circus, including Bill Powell, David Rosenwasser, and John Zamoiski; David Orr, who started the Circus Fans of America fan club in Altoona, Pennsylvania, named after me; Floyd Kruger, who, along with his esteemed committee of voters, enabled me to be inducted into the Sarasota Ring of Fame in 2012; Pat Cashin, who awarded me the Lou Jacobs Lifetime Achievement Award; The John and Mabel Ringling Museum of Art, for naming me a Sarasota Circus Celebrity; and Kathryn O'Dell, who was instrumental in my induction into the International Clown Hall of Fame in 2002.

Paul Guthiel, who documented my life and career in thousands of photographs.

Mabelle Gako Davison, for the three Hs: Help, Humor, and Hiddleston.

The directors, who allowed me to run with my ideas without running too far afield, including Richard Barstow, Paul Binder, Steve Smith, Raffaele de Ritis, Renaud Doucett, Guy Caron, Michel Barett, Eric Michael Gillette, Cal McCrystal, Peter Wallach, and Eddie Neumann.

The esteemed institutions, which have honored me by displaying my memorabilia and costumes, The John and Mabel Ringling Museum of Art in Sarasota, Florida; The International Clown Hall of Fame in Baraboo, Wisconsin; Bard College in New York City; and the Barnum Museum in Bridgeport, Connecticut

Journalists and publications who have been incredibly kind to me over the years, including The New York Times, New York Daily News, New York Post, Newsday, Boston Globe, Boston Herald, Washington Post, Bergen Record, New York Magazine, New Yorker Magazine, Wall Street Journal, People Magazine, Us Magazine, Glamour Magazine, Village Voice, Chicago Tribune, Spectacle Magazine, Cape Cod Times, Courier News, Metro, Circus Zeitung, White Tops, Jewish News, Providence Journal, Westerly Sun, Sarasota Herald Tribune, Los Angeles Times, Atlanta Journal-Constitution, Newark Star Ledger, The Press of Atlantic City, and many others.

The Today Show on NBC, Good Morning America on ABC, CBS' This Morning, and The Late Show with David Letterman for featuring me numerous times on their broadcasts, and the many local television stations in New York, Boston, Providence, Washington, Chicago, and Atlanta for doing the same.

My audience volunteers, young and old, who gave gifts to both me and their fellow audience members every day in every show by simply revealing themselves beautifully in circus rings, on stages, and on television all over the world.

My ex-wife, Roberta Lubin who not only continues to design and build my dresses, bloomers, and carpet bags, but who has also helped shape my career over our years together with her talent and great directorial eye.

My agent, Dorothee Koess, for placing me in some of the finest shows in Europe with some of the most talented people in the world, and for the legendary clown, Peter Shub, for introducing me to Dorothee.

And finally, the people who directed and ran Macy's Thanksgiving Day Parade, which for many years provided me with the biggest smiles on the biggest stage of my career, in front of millions of people on the streets of New York City and many millions more on NBC, and for giving me their "Legend of the Parade" award.

To all of you, and to the many whose names do not appear here who were so important to me over the course of my life and my career, I thank you from the bottom of my heart.

Barry Lubin's Bio

EARLY LIFE

Born July 3, 1952 in Atlantic City Hospital, Atlantic City, New Jersey.
Grew up in Ventnor, New Jersey.
Mother: Edythe Lee (Weinberg) Lubin, born March 6, 1921, Camden, New Jersey; died 2001.
Father: George Simon Lubin, born May 12, 1926, Philadelphia, Pennsylvania; died 1981.
Married Roberta Lubin, July 12, 1981; divorced 2013.
Two Children: Danielle Rose Lubin, born March 9, 1985; Emily Rita Lubin, born December 28, 1990; both born at Morristown Memorial Hospital.
Attended Atlantic City High School 1966 to 1970.
Attended Emerson College 1970 to 1973; majored in TV, Radio, Journalism (no degree).
Attended Ringling Brothers and Barnum & Bailey Clown College, 1974.

PERFORMANCES

Ringling Brothers and Barnum & Bailey Red Unit, 1975 to 1977 - US Tour.
Ringling Circus World in Haines City, Florida, 1978.
Ringling Brothers and Barnum & Bailey Blue Unit, 1978 to 1979 - US Tour.
Stand-up comedy in Los Angeles, San Diego, Boston, New York, various years; Headlined at stand-up comedy club, 2013 - Stuttgart, Germany.
Big Apple Circus, 1982 to 1987, 1989 to 1992, 1994 to 1998, 2001 to 2012 (25 seasons).
Disneyland, Los Angeles - Featured Performer, 1987 and 1988.
Powerhouse Theatre - "A Coupla Guys Who Gotta Do a Show," Santa Monica, California, 1988 (with Dick Monday).
Performed (Special Guest Artist) at Garden Brothers Circus, Vidbel's Olde Tyme Circus, Royal Hanneford Circus, Yankee Doodle Circus, Hamid Circus, L.A. Circus, Circus Sarrasani, Aachen

Winter Circus, Circus Sarasota, Limburgs Kerstcircus Holland, Circus Flora - Various years.
"Pass the Popcorn" - DeCapo Opera Theatre New York (with Dick Monday).
"Goof Family Christmas Special" – New York Goofs, ArcLight Theatre, New York City.

SPECIAL CREDITS AND PERFORMANCES

Mayor's Arts and Culture Awards, 2009, 2010, 2011, by special invitation of New York City Mayor Michael Bloomberg; performances with Mayor Bloomberg, Meryl Streep, Alec Baldwin.
International Circus Festival of Hungary, 2006 (Special Prize).
Circo Massimo Television - Rome, Italy (RAI). 2007 and 2011, "Stars en Der Manege" – Television, 2008 (8 countries).
Circus Krone Wintercircus, March 2008 (2nd American Clown in their 80 year history).
International Circus Festival of Monte Carlo, 1977 and 2008, (Special Prizes); CBS and Television Worldwide.
International Clown Festival of Taiwan - Featured Solo Show.
Kleines Fest - Germany 2008, 2010, 2013 (With Ann Hageus in 2013).
"America Meets Sweden" - Featured Festival Performance with Ann Hageus, 2012.
International Circus Festival of Moscow, 2011 (Special Prize - Great Moscow State Circus).
International Circus Festival of Izhevsk, 2012 (Special Prize of the Circus of Northern Siberia).
International Circus Festival of Kazakhstan, 2013 (Prize - Bronze Horse).
Carnegie Hall - New York City (charity performance with New York Goofs).
Radio City Music Hall - New York City (AARP Special Performance).
Town Hall - New York City (charity performance).
City Center - New York City (charity performance).
The Box New York City Nightclub - (Private Performance).
Charity Performance at Shubert Theatre - Broadway (with Chris

Meloni).
Created, Executive Produced (with Yvette Kaplan), and Starred in two television pilots for Nickelodeon Network 2006 (Oops and Daisy and Oops Makes the Bed).
Directed and wrote comedy segments for Circus of the Stars (CBS) three seasons.
Four Appearances on The Late Show with David Letterman (CBS), various years.
Appearances in the films Big Top Pee-Wee (Paramount), My Life (Columbia Pictures), Twins (Universal Pictures), Alice (Orion Pictures, dir. Woody Allen).
Featured two times in the series, Evening at Pops' (PBS).
Featured in the miniseries Circus (Show of Force Productions) PBS, Discovery Channel Worldwide).
Featured in Highlights of Ringling Brothers and Barnum & Bailey Circus, NBC 1975, 1977.
Principal Actor, Independent film, Just Married.
Principal Actor, Challenge of the Unknown, Worldwide Syndicated Series.
Principal Actor, McGraw Hill Educational Series.
Principal Actor, Towers Watson Consulting, Instructional Film.
Principal Actor, Orlando, Florida Tourism Board Film.
Principal Actor, New York City, What is Chris Meloni Doing Now?
Principal Actor, ADT Commercial.
Principal Actor, Big Apple Circus Commercial, various years.
NBC's Broadcast of Macy's Thanksgiving Day Parade – fifteen times.
NBC's Today Show – eighteen times.
ABC's Good Morning America – seven times.
CBS' This Morning – five times.
Featured on CBS' Sunday Morning.
Principal Actor, Circus of the Stars, (CBS) with Alex Karras.
The Montel Williams Show.
The Maurie Povich Show.
Martha Stewart's The Apprentice (NBC).
The Wendy Williams Show (Syndicated)
Fox News Network (Neil Cavuto Show)

Featured on HBO Special, The Big Apple Circus (1990).

TEACHING/CONSULTING/DIRECTING
Taught at Ringling Brothers and Barnum & Bailey Clown College. 1976, 1977, 1990-1997.
Creative Consultant for Cheers (NBC Television).
Creative Consultant for My Super Ex-Girlfriend (New Regency Pictures).
Creative Consultant and writer for Circus of the Stars (CBS Television).
Creative Consultant and Comedy Director for Black and White TV (MTV-Music Videos).
Creative Consultant and Director of Clowning for Big Apple Circus (14 seasons).
Director, Big Apple Circus Special Performances, Stamford, Connecticut; three years.
Interport Lecturer: Semester at Sea, Summer Voyages, 2008 and 2010.
Artist in Residence: Semester at Sea Fall Voyage, 2012 (Physical Comedy).
Special Instructor: Accademia Dell'Arte, Arezzo, Italy (Clowning/Physical Comedy).
Master Clown Workshop for Kulturkraft/Manegen, Stockholm, Sweden (funded by EU).
Clown Workshop for Hospital Clowns of Sweden.
Clown Workshops and Guest Lecturer: University of Virginia; Northwestern University; Goodman School of Drama; Shenandoah University; New York University; Emerson College.

AWARDS
Lou Jacobs Lifetime Achievement Award, 2007.
International Clown Hall of Fame Inductee, 2002.
Named Sarasota Circus Celebrity, 2010.
Circus Ring of Fame Inductee, 2012 (First Ringling Clown College Inductee).
Legend of the Parade Award - Macy's Thanksgiving Day Parade, 2012 (Fifth Award in Parade History).

MUSEUM EXHIBITS
John and Mabel Ringling Museum of Art - Sarasota, Florida (Permanent).
International Clown Hall of Fame - Baraboo, Wisconsin (Permanent).
Bard College - New York City (Nine-month exhibition).
Barnum Museum - Bridgeport, Ct. (Permanent).

www.ingramcontent.com/pod-product-compliance
Lightning Source LLC
Chambersburg PA
CBHW032043090426
42744CB00004B/102